UNVEILING ETERNITY

A Simple and Concise Approach to a Pre-Tribulation View of End Times

JOY KARANICK ROACH

WESTBOW
PRESS®
A DIVISION OF THOMAS NELSON
& ZONDERVAN

This book is a work of non-fiction. Unless otherwise noted, the author and the publisher
make no explicit guarantees as to the accuracy of the information contained in this book
and in some cases, names of people and places have been altered to protect their privacy.

WestBow Press books may be ordered through booksellers or by contacting:

WestBow Press
A Division of Thomas Nelson & Zondervan
1663 Liberty Drive
Bloomington, IN 47403
www.westbowpress.com
844-714-3454

Scripture taken from the King James Version of the Bible.

ISBN: 978-1-6642-0261-0 (sc)
ISBN: 978-1-6642-0262-7 (hc)
ISBN: 978-1-6642-0260-3 (e)

Library of Congress Control Number: 2020916006

Print information available on the last page.

WestBow Press rev. date: 09/26/2020

DEDICATION

This book is dedicated to Lois Busby, my late mom's long time friend and prayer partner. Thank you for your meticulous review and feedback in the midst of all your current circumstances. Your heart to serve the Lord inspires me.

ACKNOWLEDGEMENT

My profound appreciation to my beloved husband,
Stephen D. Roach. We labor together as we endeavor to fulfill God's
will and purpose in our lives.
You are a blessing to me beyond what I ever
prayed for and dreamed possible.

Thank you to Patti and Sue.

Thank you to all my family and friends who
encouraged me and supported this work.

CONTENTS

INTRODUCTION

We often hear people talk about the end of time as if that is the end for us. Actually, it is the beginning of our eternity. What is meant by eternity and where is it found in the Bible? Eternity is what exists outside of time, it means infinite and unending. When time ends, eternity begins and will continue forever and ever. Apostle Paul spoke to it in Philippians 1:21-24 and First Thessalonians 4: 13-18. The word *"eternity"* in English is only mentioned once in the King James Version Bible (Isaiah 57:15). In Hebrew it is the word *"ad "*. There are forty-nine references that have been translated as everlasting, end, ever, evermore, old, perpetually. However the terms *"eternal life"*, *"everlasting life"*, and *"for ever and ever"* are mentioned numerous times throughout the scriptures.

REFERENCED SCRIPTURES

† Isaiah 57:15, *"For thus saith the high and lofty One that inhabiteth eternity, whose name is Holy; I dwell in the high and holy place, with him also that is of a contrite and humble spirit, to revive the spirit of the humble, and to revive the heart of the contrite ones."*

† Philippians 1:21-24, *"21For to me to live is Christ, and to die is gain. 22 But if I live in the flesh, this is the fruit of my labour: yet what I shall choose I wot not. 23 For I am in a strait betwixt two, having a desire to depart, and to be with Christ; which is far better: 24 Nevertheless to abide in the flesh is more needful for you."*

† First Thessalonians 4:13-18, *"13 But I would not have you to be ignorant, brethren, concerning them which are asleep, that ye sorrow not, even as others which have no hope. 14For if we believe that Jesus died and rose again, even so them also which sleep in Jesus will God bring with him. ¹⁵For this we say unto you by the word of the Lord, that we which are alive and remain unto the coming of the Lord shall not prevent them which are asleep.¹⁶For the Lord himself shall descend from heaven with a shout, with the voice of the archangel, and with the trump of God: and the dead in Christ shall rise first: ¹⁷Then we which are alive and remain shall be caught up together with them in the clouds, to meet the Lord in the air: and so shall we ever be with the Lord. ¹⁸Wherefore comfort one another with these words."*

When this current heaven and earth have served their purpose, life in this world will be over but our eternal life begins. Where we spend our eternity is a choice we make in our natural or current life on earth. That sounds abstract yet it is our reason for living. We are given an opportunity in this life to choose where we will spend our eternal life. God makes every effort to reveal Himself to us so that we will choose Him and choose life.

God is patient. His wrath and destruction are His last resort. God spoke the world into existence and He will end this world by devastation. Jesus Christ, the incarnate manifestation of the Lord God Almighty was born of a virgin purposed to bring salvation to a sinful people. On that Palm Sunday before His death and resurrection, Jesus rode in on a donkey as a humble King of Peace and Redemption. However, upon His return He will come in vengeance and His wrath will bring ultimate justice. He has prepared a better place for those who love and obey His will. For those who deny Christ, He has prepared an eternal place of fire and brimstone.

† Matthew 21:5, *"Tell ye the daughter of Sion, Behold, thy King cometh unto thee, meek, and sitting upon an ass, and a colt the foal of an ass."*

† John 14:1-3, *"¹Let not your heart be troubled: ye believe in God, believe also in me. ²In my Father's house are many mansions: if it were not so, I would have told you. I go to prepare a place for you. ³And if I go and prepare a place for you, I will come again, and receive you unto myself; that where I am, there ye may be also."*

† Revelation 21:8, *"But the fearful, and unbelieving, and the abominable, and murderers, and whoremongers, and sorcerers, and*

idolaters, and all liars, shall have their part in the lake which burneth with fire and brimstone: which is the second death."

Difficult to hear? Of course! Yet, God has given us the road map. He has given us the choice. We alone must choose our path. It is not abstract, conceptual, unintelligent, or foolish. It is real! It is truth!

Many people seem hesitant to read the Bible and especially the book of Revelation for one reason or another. Some say they don't believe it, some say they are afraid, while others say they just can't understand it. I fell into the latter. I just couldn't understand Revelation. Hence, I began my study years ago and it continues as a long learning process. First, I called a friend who is an expert on the book and I asked for 'one on one' lessons. She was amazing and helped me tremendously. Eschatology is the study of end times, death and eternal things. She has written a workbook with an instructor's guide on an introduction to eschatology. Mary L. Page calls her work *Blessings in the Book: A Study Guide for the Book of Revelation*. I needed simple and straightforward information and she sat with me for hours upon hours pouring into me and giving all that she had.

I realized that I was not the only one who couldn't understand the events of the end times. I discovered that the end times are referenced throughout the Bible, not just in the Book of Revelation. Also, the end time events are not written in chronological order. They are scattered throughout creating yet another level of difficulty.

Another guide that helped me tremendously is a brochure *The Revelation of Jesus Christ: A Panorama of Prophecy* by Dr. David Jeremiah and the Turning Point Ministry. It is a brilliant visual of the sequence of the end time events.

A third helpful guide was *A Tribulation Map* by Leon Bates and can be found on *www.bbea.org*. Look for English Tribulation Map under the resources tab.

The objective of this work is to provide a simple introduction in a concrete, organized, and linear approach for those who struggle as they seek to understand. Copious amounts of information exist on this topic but without a basic introduction one can become totally overwhelmed. I believe this book will organize the information in a fundamental and concise fashion that it will incite your desire for further study. My purpose is not to explain every event in its totality. Rather, I intend to provide a succinct introduction to aid your deeper search and study. In other words, I wish this to be step one to many steps into your study of the end times. I have provided several recommendations for further study and multiple resources to assist you.

I have chosen to examine one view, the Pre-Tribulation view, because this is my belief and understanding of scripture. However, even within this view, there are many opposing views.

For those of us who find it difficult to travel back and forth between the Bible and a book trying to locate the Scripture and then finding the place in the book again, I have supported my comments with the Scriptures referenced written directly into the text. The bullet statements marked with a cross indicate a Biblical quote from a referenced Bible verse placed directly into the text. Hopefully this will make it easier to quickly read without having to flip back and forth from the Bible to this book.

Reading the Word of God will always be a learning experience and a never-ending study of faith and understanding. Enjoy your journey.

RECOMMENDED ACTIVITIES

1. Read the Book of Revelation at least once.
2. Locate the brochure *The Revelation of Jesus Christ: A Panorama of Prophecy* by Dr. David Jeremiah. Read and meditate upon it.
3. Find the Tribulation map on www.bbea.org and read it.

PERSONAL NOTES

CHAPTER ONE

BLESSING

How could anyone be afraid to read the book of Revelation? Revelation 1:3 expresses there is a blessing in reading, hearing, and keeping these words of prophecy.

† Revelation 1:3, *"Blessed is he that readeth, and they that hear the words of this prophecy, and keep those things which are written therein: for the time is at hand."*

The word *blessed* is the Greek word *'makarios'* in Strong's Exhaustive Concordance #3107***. It is important to note that the New Testament was written in Greek so we must understand the English translated words in their original language. Translated from the Greek to English as blessed or happy this word seems very straightforward and simplistic until we study the word further. It gives the implication that God extends His benefits to you or that believers are in a fortunate position to receive God's blessing. God generously gives His grace and favor toward you.

The word *'makarios'* is used fifty times in the New Testament and seven times in the book of Revelation: Revelation 1:3; 14:13; 16:15; 19:9; 20:6; 22:7; and 22:14. Matthew and Luke use the word often in their

Gospels. John uses it twice, but Mark does not use it at all. Why is that important? First, a basic understanding of how words are used gives the reader better idea of what the scripture is really saying. Secondly, it allows the reader to fully explore how the word is used throughout the scriptures. That allows for comparison and contrast, as well as, identification of common threads and patterns. Thirdly, it encourages the reader to ask questions. A question like, "Why did John use the word and Mark did not?" or "What is the significance?" may prompt a more in depth study of a concept or idea.

We often think of being blessed as having riches or being powerful. However, when Matthew reflects on the words of Jesus used in the beatitudes, he refers to those who are not at the top but at the bottom. Matthew 5:5 reads, "Blessed are the meek: for they shall inherit the earth." A chart at the end of this chapter displays the beatitudes of Matthew and the blessings of Revelation.

Blessed (makarios) is an adjective not a verb. It describes a state of joy and freedom, a state of enjoyment and well-being that does not depend on our circumstances. It describes freedom from daily worries and care because our circumstances are in His hands. That is a blessing.

As you read the book of Revelation, remember this Divine blessing. For believers, knowing the outcome of repentance and living a righteous life is that you are in His care and you need not worry. You have assurance knowing the Almighty God favors you, watches over you, guides, leads, and provides for you. You experience an inner state of bliss and peace for yourself but a resilient concern for those who don't know God.

There is yet another blessing you acquire while reading the Book of Revelation. We recognize the purpose of Revelation reveals the person, power, and plan of Jesus Christ. Revelation tells us so much about who Jesus is. There is a blessing in knowing Jesus personally. I have found at least twenty-three descriptions of Jesus. Here are a few of them. He is called *Jesus Christ* in Revelation 1:1. He is the *Root of David* in 5:5, the *Lion of Judah* in 5:5, the *Slain Lamb* in 5:6, the *Angry Lamb* in 6:16-17, and the *Tender Lamb* in 7:17. He is the *Faithful Witness* in Revelation 1:5. He is the *Alpha and Omega* in 1:8. He is the *King of Kings and the Lord of Lords* in 19:16, and the *Faithful and True* in Revelation 19:11. This is only a partial listing. One of the activities for you is to find at least twenty-three descriptions of Jesus in the Book of Revelation. You will need resources to help you do this. One is the Strong's Exhaustive Concordance.

What is a Strong's Exhaustive Concordance?

***Strong's Exhaustive Concordance is a book written by James Strong, which lists every word of the King James Bible and every time it appears. The scripture for each reference is listed on the sideline. The reason is because the English word in one verse may be a totally different Greek or Hebrew word in another verse. Remember that the original languages of the Bible are Greek and Hebrew and some Aramaic. The exhaustive concordance means that it provides the original Hebrew or Greek definition for each word. A number is assigned to each word also on the side. That number is used to locate the word in the original Hebrew or Greek in the dictionaries found in the back of the book. If it is not an exhaustive concordance, such as the one in the back of your Bible, there will be no Greek or Hebrew definitions and usually it will not be a complete list of each word of the Bible and each time it occurs.

It will look something like this order:

The Word	Book and Verse	Strong's #
Part of the verse written out with the word abbreviated. Only the first letter of the word is written.	Reference	1.Italicized means it is Greek and Not Italicized means it is Hebrew. 2. Old Testament references are in the Hebrew and the New Testament references are in the Greek.
High And all the *h* hills that were	Gen 7:9	1364
Rather But *r*rejoice, because your names (The words of Jesus are sometimes highlighted)	Luke 10:20	*3123*

***(Other concordances are used for other versions such as the NIV Bible. Not all versions have a corresponding concordance. I use the KJV accompanying Strong's Concordance since he was the first to do this work and it is more familiar. I study with many versions of the Bible but when I look up words in the original language I start here. This is why I used KJV in this book but you will want to read other versions.

BEATITUDES COMPARED
REVELATION & MATTHEW

Notice from this chart the blessings in Revelation compared to the beatitudes or blessings in Matthew.

#	SCRIPTURE KJV	BEATITUDE	SCRIPTURE KJV	BEATITUDE
1	REV. 1:3	Blessed is he that readeth, and they that hear the words of this prophecy, and keep those things which are written therein: for the time is at hand.	MATTHEW 5:3	Blessed are the poor in spirit: for theirs is the kingdom of heaven.
2	REV. 14:13	And I heard a voice from heaven saying unto me, Write, Blessed are the dead which die in the Lord from henceforth: Yea, saith the Spirit, that they may rest from their labours; and their works do follow them.	MATTHEW 5:4	Blessed are they that mourn: for they shall be comforted.
3	REV. 16:15	Behold, I come as a thief. Blessed is he that watcheth, and keepeth his garments, lest he walk naked, and they see his shame.	MATTHEW 5:5	Blessed are the meek: for they shall inherit the earth.
4	REV. 19:9	And he saith unto me, Write, Blessed are they which are called unto the marriage supper of the Lamb. And he saith unto me, These are the true sayings of God.	MATTHEW 5:6	Blessed are they which do hunger and thirst after righteousness: for they shall be filled.
5	REV. 20:6	Blessed and holy is he that hath part in the first resurrection: on such the second death hath no power, but they shall be priests of God and of Christ, and shall reign with him a thousand years.	MATTHEW 5:7	Blessed are the merciful: for they shall obtain mercy.
6	REV. 22:7	Behold, I come quickly: blessed is he that keepeth the sayings of the prophecy of this book.	MATTHEW 5:8	Blessed are the pure in heart: for they shall see God.
7	REV. 22:14	Blessed are they that do his commandments that they may have right to the tree of life, and may enter in through the gates into the city.	MATTHEW 5:9	Blessed are the peacemakers: for they shall be called the children of God.
8			MATTHEW 5:10	Blessed are they which are persecuted for righteousness' sake: for theirs is the kingdom of heaven.

RECOMMENDED ACTIVITIES

1. Obtain a Strong's Exhaustive Concordance, read and study on how to use the concordance. There are instructions for the reader in the front of the book. The concordance can also be found on the Internet but in a different format than the book. You can usually find concordances that are very inexpensive at a second hand or thrift store.

2. Locate and browse the following websites, which are great resources for study.
   https://www.biblestudytools.com/
   https://biblehub.com/
   https://www.studylight.org/
   https://www.biblegateway.com/

3. Find the word *blessed* in the Greek. Meditate on your blessings as you read the Book of Revelation.

4. Find and list at least twenty-three descriptions of Jesus in the Book of Revelation.

PERSONAL NOTES

CHAPTER TWO

INTERPRETING REVELATION

Reading and understanding Scripture requires application and utilization of certain principles of interpretation. One could write an entire book on this topic and many have. The purpose of this chapter is to provide a very brief introduction of Biblical interpretation. The main idea of interpreting Scripture involves closing the gaps of time by understanding the intent of the original author and hearing as an original hearer. This field of study embraces three areas: exegesis, hermeneutics, and homiletics. Only exegesis and hermeneutics are pertinent for the intention of this work unless you are a Pastor or educator of the Word. Homiletics deals more with the application rather than the interpretation. It gathers from the interpretation to formulate an application and conclusion. Homiletics in its simplest form is the art of preparing the sermon and preaching plans based on what has been discovered. It touches on how to write the sermon and explores various approaches to preaching. For the purpose of this book the focus will be an overview of exegesis and hermeneutics.

EXEGESIS

Biblical exegesis is the critical interpretation and explanation of the Bible to find its intended meaning by its original author. Critical, in this sense, means an intensive and extensive evaluation or analysis. Prayerfully approaching the Word and followed by reading the passage multiple times is the first and foremost important part of exegesis. Interpretation of the Bible cannot be done without the Holy Spirit alongside of the reader. Prayerfully meditating on the passage is equally as important. After which exegesis can commence.

Through exegesis, the interpreter seeks to uncover the literal meaning of the text and reveal the intention of the author. Exegesis tries to make sense of what the text meant to the original writer and hearer and then apply it to today's audience and situation. Asking questions is critical to understanding the Word of God. In other words, asking questions like when was this written? Who wrote it? Why did he write it? What did Moses mean when he wrote Exodus 34:10-11? What does the word marvels/wonders mean? Who were all of those "ites"? How did they live? Where did they live? Where is their country today? Were they related? Where else in Scripture are they mentioned? Why and how? What did Dr. Luke mean when he wrote Acts 3:1-10? Why does it say Peter and John and not some other disciples? What is the meaning of their names? What is their symbolic impression? Could Peter represent the church? Could John represent love? What if the church and love walked together? Is this the temple where Jesus went? Did Jesus see the lame man when He was on earth? Why was he healed now and not before? What is the gate called beautiful? Where is it today? Is it a real gate? What does it mean to be lame? How long was he lame? How old was he? What did Apostle John mean when he penned Revelation 3:1? Did God really have seven spirits? What does that mean? What does angel mean? What does a particular word mean in the Hebrew or Greek? Why did the author use one word instead of another word? Why was the author the only one to use a specific word found in Scripture? How many times was that word used? How would the Hebrew people have understood the creation in Genesis when Moses wrote it? Or did Moses write it? How much did Goliath's armor weigh? What is meant by a shekel and how much is that today? What does in the month of Adar mean?

A serious student of the Word will not merely read without asking questions and seeking answers to the questions. The answers lead to understanding and personal application.

There is a method to guide the question and the study. One cannot solely read the passage and think they know what is meant. A deeper study is necessary. Have you ever listened to a speaker and there seems to be no flow or little study prior to delivery? Rather, it seems there are just a lot of thoughts without a big idea or connection point? You have heard it said, "Oh the Holy Spirit will tell me when I get up to preach what to say." Yes that is true. The Holy Spirit can also guide your study and speak during preparation or exegesis. Of course there is what we call a "Rhema Word" such as when a particular Scripture penetrates your Spirit in an extraordinary way. The Holy Spirit illuminates the Word during study and during meditation. God speaks when and how He wants to speak. Exegesis is not talking about a "Rhema Word". Exegesis intends for us to breakout the passage and analyze it from various perspectives. Look at the passage as if you were twirling a diamond around in your hand so that you could determine its color, its weight, clarity and all of its properties. Imagine the passage as a puzzle where each word or phrase is broken apart and thereby you have to put it back together. There are four areas of concentration that are called gaps or context: language, history, culture and geography. I also think of them as different windows to look through when studying the Word. Look through four different windows of your residence. You see different views and get different insights. Do the same with Scripture.

I. LANGUAGE

The Bible was originally written in primarily two languages. The Old Testament was written in Hebrew and the New Testament was written in Greek. A few passages and words can be found in the Aramaic language. Our Bibles have been translated from those languages. Although our English Bible does a good job of translating, often the meaning doesn't get exposed as it would in the time of its writing. There may be a nuance about it that needs to be understood. This is why Bible Scholars must take Hebrew and Greek language and grammar in school. Everyone cannot go to seminary and learn these languages. Ah, there is good news. Most scholars like to write. One scholar named James Strong wrote *Strong's Exhaustive Concordance of the Bible*. We discussed this in the first chapter. Commentaries are another resource available by the thousands. Many are online. Preachers who are trained will often provide information related to the text as well. This is a good reason to go to church or listen to good preachers on the radio or TV.

Commentaries are comments from the scholar. It is important to know who is giving his or her comments. It is important to know something about the author's background and when they wrote. Many commentators will analyze a word or phrase in its original language and will share certain distinctions about it that can make the Scripture come alive. Many word studies have been done online and these can be most helpful. Simply type in word study on what word it is you are interested in studying. Resources such as Bible Dictionaries, Bible Handbooks, Theological Workbooks, and Lexicons are of tremendous assistance. Every personal library can benefit from a good selection of these resources. Thrift stores often have many of these books and sell them at a very low cost.

2. HISTORY

Consideration of the historical context is necessary in order to interpret the text. The history of Israel and the history of Christianity are just two examples critical to understanding the Word of God. However, there is more, which is essential to a deeper understanding.

Have you ever asked yourself what happened during the four hundred years of silence between the Old and New Testaments? Did you know that the blank page of your Bible separating the two Testaments has so much history written on it? Not literally on that page but it gives a nice visual to imagine four hundred years of history on a page. Did you ever ask why Pharisees and Sadducees were not mentioned in the Old Testament? How did they suddenly appear in the New? What brought them about? How about this one? Why was the New Testament written in Greek? Why did they not continue writing in Hebrew? Something happened during those 400 years of history on that blank page that impacted the world and the language of the world. Those four hundred years called the Intertestamental period helped to prepare the way of the Lord! Consider this! Why was Jonah, in the Old Testament, so bitter toward the people God told him to minister? Why would a prophet and seasoned man of God refuse to do what God told him? Maybe the answer is in history. Who ruled over Nineveh in the years before and up to Jonah's day? How did they treat Israel? The kings acted like the terrorists of our time. Those Assyrians, Gentiles; they were known for their cruelty and ruthlessness. They literally cut off hands and feet, took off noses, ears and lips. God called Jonah to go and tell them He loved them and wanted them experience His love. Today God is telling us to go to the world, the murderers, the drug addicted, the terrorists and tell them that God loves them and He wants them to experience His love. Will you go?

See how history helps us to look at yesterday and see what God is saying to us today. Don't panic! There are resources available to make this easy and fun. The Internet is loaded with information that makes it simple to search and focus on one portion of history instead of reading a whole book at a time. Sites like the following are packed with great information.

http://timeline.biblehistory.com/home
https://sacred-texts.com/
https://www.bible-history.com/
http://jewishencyclopedia.com/
https://www.jewishvirtuallibrary.org/
https://www.biblegateway.com/
https://biblehub.com/
https://www.biblestudytools.com/
https://www.studylight.org

Bible timeline charts are particularly easy and quick to read and comprehend. Many of them include the Biblical and secular history. If you enjoy reading, look for books on the history of Israel or the history of Christianity. Some are quite large and intimidating but interesting and helpful. Many are online as well or can be found also in thrift stores. 1. *Rose Book of Bible Charts, Maps & Timelines*, 2. *Holman Book of Biblical Chart, Maps, and Reconstructions*, 3. *Christian History Made Easy*, offer a wealth of information.

Josephus was a first century historian. His complete works are in a book that bears his name. *Josephus* is a must for every believer's library.

3. CULTURE

Our society is blessed with a diversity of people. Most people travel to some degree throughout the USA and other countries. We have some idea of how different cultures experience or view the world. What we may not know is what was culture like during Bible days. What was the custom to *gird your loins like a man* in Job 38:3? Check out https://www.artofmanliness.com/articles/how-to-gird-up-your-loins-an-illustrated-guide/ to see the procedure. Can you now understand Job 38:3 better? We are at war! Gird up.

Questions like these are important to grasp the idea of culture in the Bible. What was bread and bread making like during Bible times? What is its significance? Why was it on the Table of Showbread in the tabernacle? How does the Table of Showbread point us to Jesus? What was the Table of Showbread used for? What were the marriage customs of the day when Jesus turned the water into wine (John 2)? What would a marriage feast look like in the time of Jesus? How does that connect to Revelation for us today?

What kind of trades and professions existed during Bible times? What was the work of a potter in Jeremiah 18? How does that relate to us? The process demonstrates how the potter gathers, cleans, shapes (throws) the clay then dries and fires the vessel just like Jesus does to make us a perfect clay and beautiful piece of pottery.

If the culture is not understood then the meaning of the Scripture cannot be understood. Resources that support understanding culture during Bible days is found using words like manners and customs of Bible times, Bible lands and Bible life. The Internet is a great source for especially when searching specific topics.

You will want to also include some Jewish resources. We are Judeo-Christian so we want to seek understanding of Hebrew thought. There are many Jewish traditions in the Bible; the feasts, the calendar, and Jewish customs to name a few. What do they mean and when do they occur? What does it mean for Christians? For example, Esther 3:7, "In the first month, that *is*, the month Nisan, in the twelfth year of king Ahasuerus, they cast Pur, that *is*, the lot, before Haman from day to day, and from month to month, *to* the twelfth *month*, that *is*, the month Adar." What are the months of Nisan and Adar? What feast was celebrated in this month? What is the significance? How does it point us to Jesus? If I said to you "in the month of December" immediately thoughts and pictures of Christmas, end of year activities, winter, and children out of school would flood your mind. The same should be when we read the Bible. A good resource to study the Jewish months, feasts, and customs is necessary. There are many wonderful online resources.

http://www.jewfaq.org/calendar.htm
https://hebrew4christians.com/Holidays/Introduction/introduction.html
https://www.timeanddate.com/calendar/jewish-calendar.html

Another resource is The Talmud, which comprises the Mishna and the Gemara. It is a compilation of many ancient Hebrew Biblical teachings. Remember the Jews did not originally have a written Word. It was passed down orally. So this book is full of Jewish laws, ethics, customs, and history. The Gemara portion is commentary or discussion on the Mishna. The Midrash serves as yet another Jewish exposition or interpretive resource. One book I like is *Jewish Literacy* written by Rabbi Joseph Telushkin. It makes for interesting reading and comparison between Hebraic thought and western thought. The purpose of studying these alongside of the Bible is to gain understanding, to compare, to contrast and to appreciate how God has worked in the past, now, and in the future.

5. GEOGRAPHY

Geography means land description. It describes the land, its features, and its interactions. Thank goodness we don't have to take this course in order to understand the Bible. However, when we read a Scripture in which a place is mentioned we want to know something about it. We must ask questions when reading the Word! What does this name mean? Does it still have the same name? Where is it on the map? What about its terrain? Is it mountainous or a valley, a desert or wetlands? Is it near the sea or inland? The Bible will come alive when we connect to it.

Names of the places in the Bible are not always the same today. For instance, Babylon is Iraq today. Persia is Iran. There are too many name changes to list here. World atlas, book of maps, atlas of the Bible, ancient world atlas, Biblical geography, Bible lands, or atlas with

Christian history are types of words and phrases to look for when looking for a book to search the Biblical places. Also there are many resources online. Here are just a few.

htttp://www.jewfaq.org/calendar.htm
http://www.lookinguntojesus.info/BSTopics/AncientNameswith CurrentNames.html
https://www.bibleblender.com/2015/biblical-lessons/biblical-history/list-of-bible-places-old-new-testament-biblical-locations
https://www.bible-history.com/
https://www.wogim.org/anland.htm
https://www.worldatlas.com/

Why does this make a difference in your study? The great river Euphrates is cited in Revelation 16:12. Euphrates means fruitfulness in Hebrew and the good and abounding river in Greek. It is mentioned twenty-one times in the Bible (KJV): nineteen in the Old Testament and two in the New Testament. Both times it is found in the New Testament in Revelation 9 and 16. This river will dry up during the Tribulation. Find it on the map. It separates the East and West serving as a barrier. This river flows North to South from Turkey, Syria and through Iraq and empties into the Persian Gulf. The kings of the East need to march a two hundred million-person army to the west where the Battle of Armageddon will be fought at the end of the Tribulation. Now look to the east and see which country might be large enough to have a two hundred million-person army. Its water has already begun to dry up and the snakes are slithering on dry ground and killing people.

Now study the Euphrates and learn all that you can about it. Learn its history and its wildlife. Where it is mentioned in Scripture. Who will be bound in this great river in Revelation 9? How many miles is it in length? Through what sort of terrain does it flow? What sort of vegetation is grown around it? What are some of the concerns with the river today? What significance and conclusions can you entertain?

Are your conclusions solid and grounded in the Word? Now you are just beginning to exegete the River Euphrates.

HERMENEUTICS

Exegesis goes further than looking at the above gaps discussed. Exegesis and hermeneutics are often used interchangeably because they are so closely related. There is a distinction. I like to understand it as exegesis is the research and hermeneutics is the rules, which guide the research. It is like playing golf. There must be rules in order to play the game or there is no game. Hermeneutics embodies several principles, called the principles of hermeneutics but for this purpose only a few of them will be discussed.

PRINCIPLES OF INTERPRETATION

Please remember that in this very quick chapter you are getting a small glance into the huge field of Biblical interpretation. It is important you have at least a basic understanding for Biblical study. I recommend a book that will be of tremendous help to you: *Interpreting the Scriptures: A Textbook On How To Interpret The Bible* written by Kevin J. Conner and Ken Malmin.

THE CONTEXT PRINCIPLE

A failure of most people when reading the Word of God is to not study the Scripture in its context. Scripture interprets Scripture. The meaning cannot be totally understood without considering its context or framework of a passage. A passage must be understood in the context of a chapter, a chapter to the book, and a book to the Testament. We want to interpret the Bible saying what it really says and not what we want it to say. The goal of this principle is properly and rightly dividing the Word.

We examine the Scripture placing the concept or topic in its contextual place. The goal is to link or unite the thought that runs throughout. We need to link particular scriptures in Revelation with those found in other passages of Revelation, Daniel, the Prophets and so forth. The Book of Daniel helps to unveil or unlock the door to the Book of Revelation.

One example of context is found in John 10:10, "The thief cometh not, but for to steal, and to kill, and to destroy: I am come that they might have life, and that they might have *it* more abundantly." Immediately our thought is the thief is the devil. We have heard it preached that way. Read the larger context of the passage carefully and you will readily see that those Jesus is talking about are robbers, wolves, and strangers who come to harm the sheep (10:1, 5, 8, 10, 12). Those who came before Jesus wanted to exploit the sheep but Jesus came to defend the sheep. Jesus wasn't talking about the devil in this verse. He was speaking of the false teachers and false religious leaders.

Now read Jeremiah 23 and see if you find a thread that can be woven. It begins Jeremiah 23:1, "Woe be unto the pastors that destroy and scatter the sheep of my pasture! saith the LORD."

THE COMPARISON PRINCIPLE

To compare means to consider the similarities or dissimilarities or to find the differences and likenesses between two or more things. Compare Revelation 2:7, 11, 17, 29; 3:6, 13, and 22 with Revelation 13:9. How is it alike and how is it different? The words *church and spirit* have been omitted in Revelation 13:9. What can you make of this? This will be discussed later.

Compare Bible versions. Compare the stories in the Gospels Matthew, Mark, and Luke to each other. Compare blessings and curses in Deuteronomy 28. Compare light and darkness. Compare the Egyptian plagues of Exodus 7-12 with the judgments from Revelation 6-19.

THE CHRIST CENTERED PRINCIPLE

This principle centers theologically on Christ. Christ is the center of all Scripture. Bible study should always ask how the Scripture points us to Jesus. The Old Testament pre-figures Christ. Where do you see Christ in the Old Testament? The New Testament in John 1:1 says, "In the beginning was the Word, and the Word was with God, and the Word was God." Do a survey of Revelation and identify how this book places Christ as the centerpiece. Revelation reveals more about Christ than almost any other book. He is, He was and He is to come. He is the root of David, the bright and morning star. He is the Alpha and Omega, the beginning and the end. He is the Amen. The list goes on and on and more will come on this in following chapters.

THE NUMERICAL PRINICPLE

Numbers have a significant meaning in Scripture. Believers do not practice numerology from the new age traditions or anything related to the occult. However, God placed numbers in the Bible so we cannot overlook their meaning. Biblical numbers have a meaning. There is more discussion in this chapter on the meaning of numbers.

The Hebrew Aleph-Bet (not written alphabet) serves also as the numbering system. Aleph = 1, Bet = 2 and so forth until number 10. Each letter then continues as 10, 20, 30, 40 etc. until 100 then each letter is assigned a value of 100, 200, 300, and 400 is the last number. It ends with the Aleph-Bet letter Tav as being number 400. Every word can add up to a particular number. You can actually determine the numerical value of the word and identify other words with the same value. Each value can have a deeper meaning. The Greek alphabet has a similar numbering system.

Here are some online resources.

https://menorah-bible.jimdofree.com/english/structure-of-the-bible/alphabets-and-numerical-values/
https://www.billmounce.com/greekalphabet/greek-alphabet
https://www.hebrew4christians.com/Grammar/Unit_One/Aleph-Bet/aleph-bet.html
https://www.jewishvirtuallibrary.org/the-hebrew-alphabet-aleph-bet
http://www.thewordnotes.com/numvalhg.pdf

THE GENRE PRINCIPLE

Genre means a category or a grouping. In music you have various genres. There is country, Christian, jazz, rock, and so forth. Each of those categories can actually be broken down in their sub-categories. The Bible speaks in various genres as well. The Psalms are songs. Proverbs is wisdom literature. Stories, especially in the Old Testament are narratives. Jesus spoke many times using parables. Matthew, Mark, Luke and John are the Gospels and should be interpreted harmoniously. Some books are historical in nature, like Acts, while others are epistles or letters. Often we find poetic literature in the Bible. It is imperative to know what type of literature is being read. Each genre requires interpretation from different perspectives. Revelation is an apocalyptic literature. That word will be discussed later on.

THE REVELATION OR MENTION PRINCIPLE

The Bible from the Old Testament to the end of the New Testament is an unfolding revelation. God did not reveal all His truths at one time. He initiated the revelation in Genesis, and then He moved progressively throughout the Bible until He was complete in Revelation. There are three kinds of mention principles important to examine:

1. The first mention principle, which looks at a concept, place, name, symbol, or event in Scripture from the time it was first mentioned. This principle helps to guide or lead us into a deeper truth. It helps to uncover the meaning. Suppose you had no knowledge of the Old Testament and you come across Jude 1:7 in the New Testament, "Even as Sodom and Gomorrha, and the cities about them in like manner, giving themselves over to fornication, and going after strange flesh, are set forth for an example, suffering the vengeance of eternal fire." Sodom and Gomorrha would be foreign to you and obstruct your understanding. Now search for the first mention of Sodom and Gomorrha. It can be found in Genesis 10:19, "And the border of the Canaanites was from Sidon, as thou comest to Gerar, unto Gaza; as thou goest, unto Sodom, and Gomorrah, and Admah, and Zeboim, even unto Lasha."

That really didn't help you understand what Jude 1:7 means.

2. Secondly is the progressive principle. How and where does Sodom and Gomorrah progress throughout the Scripture? Reading Genesis 18-19 will shed more light on the subject.

3. The third mention or revelation principle is decided when you consider where and how Sodom and Gomorrah was used in all of scripture. A complete revelation of the topic or idea has unfolded. The complete mention contributes to a comprehensive examination of Sodom and Gomorrah by which the whole truth will be appreciated and understood.

Consider this chart, which illustrates more fully. You can readily see the first mention of a topic and the progressive and complete mention. I have given only a part of Sodom and Gomorrah's mention. Find other scriptures related to them and construct a complete mention of that topic. Meditate and study what Apostle John's meaning is when compared to the context of other Biblical references. A concordance will help tremendously.

TOPIC	REVELATION	OTHER BIBLICAL REFERENCES
First and the Last	Revelation 1:11,17; 2:8; 22:13	Isaiah 41:4; 44:6; 48:12
Second Coming Son of Man coming in the clouds	Revelation 1:7	Daniel 7:13; Matthew 24:30; Mark 13:26; Mark 14:62; Luke 21:27
Sodom and Gomorrah	Revelation 11:8	Genesis 18-19; Genesis 18:20; Luke 10:12; Luke 17:29; Romans 9:29; Second Peter 2:6; Jude 7
Two Witnesses	Revelation 11:3-4	Zechariah 4:14

REFERENCED SCRIPTURES

FIRST AND THE LAST

✝ Isaiah 41:4, *"Who hath wrought and done it, calling the generations from the beginning? I the Lord, the first, and with the last; I am he."*

✝ Isaiah 44:6, *"Thus saith the Lord the King of Israel, and his redeemer the Lord of hosts; I am the first, and I am the last; and beside me there is no God."*

✝ Isaiah 48:12, *"Hearken unto me, O Jacob and Israel, my called; I am he; I am the first, I also am the last."*

✝ Revelation 1:11, *"Saying, I am Alpha and Omega, the first and the last: and, What thou seest, write in a book, and send it unto the seven churches which are in Asia; unto Ephesus, and unto Smyrna, and unto Pergamos, and unto Thyatira, and unto Sardis, and unto Philadelphia, and unto Laodicea."*

✝ Revelation 1:17, *"And when I saw him, I fell at his feet as dead. And he laid his right hand upon me, saying unto me, Fear not; I am the first and the last:"*

✝ Revelation 2:8, *"And unto the angel of the church in Smyrna write; These things saith the first and the last, which was dead, and is alive;"*

✝ Revelation 22:13, *"I am Alpha and Omega, the beginning and the end, the first and the last."*

SECOND COMING

✟ Daniel 7:13, *"I saw in the night visions, and, behold, one like the Son of man came with the clouds of heaven, and came to the Ancient of days, and they brought him near before him."*

✟ Matthew 24:30, *"And then shall appear the sign of the Son of man in heaven: and then shall all the tribes of the earth mourn, and they shall see the Son of man coming in the clouds of heaven with power and great glory."*

✟ Mark 13:26, *"And then shall they see the Son of man coming in the clouds with great power and glory."*

✟ Mark 14:62, *"And Jesus said, I am: and ye shall see the Son of man sitting on the right hand of power, and coming in the clouds of heaven."*

✟ Luke 21:27, *"And then shall they see the Son of man coming in a cloud with power and great glory."*

✟ Revelation 1:7, *"Behold, he cometh with clouds; and every eye shall see him, and they also which pierced him: and all kindreds of the earth shall wail because of him. Even so, Amen."*

SODOM AND GOMORRAH

✟ Genesis 18:20, *"And the Lord said, Because the cry of Sodom and Gomorrah is great, and because their sin is very grievous;"*

✟ Luke 10:12, *"But I say unto you, that it shall be more tolerable in that day for Sodom, than for that city."*

✟ Luke 17:29, *"But the same day that Lot went out of Sodom it rained fire and brimstone from heaven, and destroyed them all."*

✟ Romans 9:29, *"And as Esaias said before, Except the Lord of Sabaoth had left us a seed, we had been as Sodoma, and been made like unto Gomorrha."*

✟ Second Peter 2:6, *"And turning the cities of Sodom and Gomorrha into ashes condemned them with an overthrow, making them an ensample unto those that after should live ungodly;"*

✟ Jude 1:7, *"Even as Sodom and Gomorrha, and the cities about them in like manner, giving themselves over to fornication, and going after strange flesh, are set forth for an example, suffering the vengeance of eternal fire."*

✝ Revelation 11:8, *"And their dead bodies shall lie in the street of the great city, which spiritually is called Sodom and Egypt, where also our Lord was crucified."*

TWO WITNESSES

✝ Zechariah 4:3, *"And two olive trees by it, one upon the right side of the bowl, and the other upon the left side thereof."*

✝ Zechariah 4:11, *"Then answered I, and said unto him, What are these two olive trees upon the right side of the candlestick and upon the left side thereof?"*

✝ Zechariah 4:14, *"Then said he, These are the two anointed ones, that stand by the* Lord *of the whole earth."*

✝ Revelation 11: 3-4. *"³ And I will give power unto my two witnesses, and they shall prophesy a thousand two hundred and threescore days, clothed in sackcloth. ⁴These are the two olive trees, and the two candlesticks standing before the God of the earth."*

THE KRONOS PRINCIPLE

This principle deals with the elements of time and / or sequence of events. It deals with the time of the clock and the time of the calendar. It considers the times, seasons, periods, ages of past, present, and future, and generations. It asks a question of when is Scripture referring. Is it dealing with the end time, the present age, the age of creation, the Messianic age, or the time of Abraham, Isaac, and Jacob (the Patriarchs)? Within the future age the Tribulation Period will occur. In the latter days the Millennial Age will transpire. Revelation is speaking of a future time. However, with Christ Jesus, He is and was and is to come. There is no time with Him. He always was, is, and will be.

The Kronos principle also examines the sequence of events, times, seasons, places, and people. Ponder the events from the birth of Jesus to the death of Jesus. What was the sequence of events from the first to the seventh day of creation? Examine the Ark of the Covenant and its sequential travels. Where is it now? Do the same exercise with the tabernacle and temple. When did the tabernacle become a temple? How many temples were there? What was the sequence? What happened to the Ark, tabernacle and temple? Will there be another temple? Recognize that the Bible is not in chronological order. Revelation is not in chronological order. It moves back and forth often making it difficult to read and connect events. Charts and outlines are remarkable tools to help organize information as you read and study.

THE SYMBOLIC PRINCIPLE

Although we take the scriptures literal, Revelation uses extensive symbolic language. We accept that 144,000 Jews literally means 144,000 Jews. The division of twelve tribes and 12,000 from each tribe has a symbolic meaning in that twelve represents governmental perfection or establishment of government. The 144,000 Jews will not be a government but will be Tribulation evangelists that God will use during that time. Symbols represent thoughts, ideas or concepts that express or exemplify the meaning. Among them include numbers, colors, places, people, angels, stars and more. Some will be discussed below.

NUMBERS

E. W. Bullinger has written a phenomenal book, *Number in Scripture*, which I believe should be a part of every believer's library. It is also online. Two places you may find it are mentioned below:

http://www.biblebelievers.org.au/number01.htm and
https://philologos.org/__eb-nis/default.htm

Four often represents direction or the four corners of the earth: North, South, East and West.

Seven is found in 31 verses and 48 times in Revelation. It represents fullness, completion, and spiritual perfection. The word for seven in the Greek New Testament is *"heptah"*. In the Old Testament Hebrew it is *"shehbah"* and means to be full or satisfied, or have enough of. It also means a binding oath.

Six Six Six (666) is the mark of the beast (Revelation 13:18). Three score is sixty and one score equals twenty. Six is the number of man. Man was created on the sixth day of creation.

> † Revelation 13:18, *"Here is wisdom. Let him that hath understanding count the number of the beast: for it is the number of a man; and his number is Six hundred threescore and six."*

One hundred and forty-four thousand (144,000) are the number of Jews, twelve thousand from each tribe, marked with the seal of God. Notice the tribe of Dan is missing. No one really knows why but there are many theories and assumptions. This tribe committed so much idolatry perhaps that is why it is left out here and also in First Chronicles 1-9. There are many good articles on the Internet that are interesting to read on it. The 144,000 are called servants of God and are kept safe from the terror during the Tribulation. They are Tribulation evangelists.

Ten (one hundred, thousand, ten thousand all multiples and degrees of ten) is a number of ordinal perfection and completion. Ten may also mean a short time.

Three- and one-half years = forty-two months=1260 days represents half of the Tribulation. The Great Tribulation marks the other half of The Tribulation Period when judgments will greatly intensify. The middle of the Tribulation is when the Antichrist will reveal himself.

Twelve is another perfect number representing governmental perfection. Consider the twelve tribes of Israel, the twelve sons of Jacob, the twelve sons of Ishmael, the twelve disciples and the twenty-four elders who are twelve times two.

PARTIAL LIST OF SYMBOLS IN REVELATION

SYMBOL	MEANING AND COMMENTS
Abyss	• Bottomless pit • Hell • Deep boundless space • Underworld
Babylon	• Idolatry and religious confusion • Departure of the faith • City of Satan • Headquarters of Antichrist • Can represent Rome as in First Peter 5:13
Beast	• Antichrist, Kingdom, World Government • Antichrist arises seemingly out of the Mediterranean Sea • It may mean a personal antichrist or an institution such as the Roman Empire.
Black	• Death, sin, apostasy (defection of the belief)
Church/es	• Seven churches representing bodies of Christians in seven Asian localities. • The universal church • Mentioned twenty times in Revelation occurring in chapters 2-3 except one mention in Revelation 22:16.
Dragon	• Satan
Four Horses	• Horse means war • White- conquering; Bow- signifies a warrior and violence; Crown- indicates a ruler, leader, head of state • Fiery Red- bloodshed; Take peace from the earth; Weapon of Sword- killing and slaughter • Black- famine and pestilence, grief, mourning, economic disaster; Scales- tool of measuring wheat and barley • Pale- Death and Hades; Weapons of sword, hunger, death and beasts of the earth
Lamb	• Jesus • Sacrificial Lamb
Mystery Babylon	• Wife of the Antichrist (mimics the Bride of Christ)
Right hand	• Position of Authority
Seven Heads	• Seven world governments

Seven Mountains or Hills	• The Kingdoms of the world governments • Political strength • Rome is often called the city of seven hills
Stars	• Messengers, Angels
Ten crowns	• Divisions of the last world government • Last of the seven world governments believed by many to be the United Nations, which will divide into ten divisions.
Ten Horns	• Ten leaders who will rule with the Antichrist • Ten Kings
Throne	• The place of judgment • The royal seat of God
Trumpets	• Warning • Military strength, Authority • Announcing New Moon or Jubilee Year or some memorial
Twenty four elders	• A group of redeemed from the earth • Bible does not reveal their identity • Various debates as to who they are
Two Witnesses	• Two prophets that will prophesy for 1260 days during the Tribulation • Bible does not identify them • Many speculate if they are Moses and Elijah or Elijah and Enoch
Wine	• Usually represents the Holy Spirit but in Revelation 14:8 symbolizes forced false belief and doctrines of the world • Demonic control

NAMES OF JESUS IN REVELATION

ALPHA AND OMEGA - (Revelation 1:8, 11; 21:6; 22:13) Alpha is the first (beginning) letter of the Greek alphabet while Omega is the last (end). Jesus is the first and the last and everything in between. He is the beginning and the end Revelation 1:8. Notice **Alpha and Omega**, the **First and the Last,** and the **Beginning and the End** appear in the beginning of Revelation and also at the end of Revelation.

ALMIGHTY (Revelation 1:8)

✝ Revelation 1:8, *"I am Alpha and Omega, the beginning and the ending, saith the Lord, which is, and which was, and which is to come, the Almighty."*

✝ Revelation 1:11, *"Saying, I am Alpha and Omega, the first and the last: and, What thou seest, write in a book, and send it unto the seven churches which are in Asia; unto Ephesus, and unto Smyrna, and unto Pergamos, and unto Thyatira, and unto Sardis, and unto Philadelphia, and unto Laodicea."*

✝ Revelation 21:6, *"And he said unto me, It is done. I am Alpha and Omega, the beginning and the end. I will give unto him that is athirst of the fountain of the water of life freely."*

✝ Revelation 22:13, *"I am Alpha and Omega, the beginning and the end, the first and the last."*

AMEN, THE is Jesus, the faithful and true witness (Revelation 3:14). The word amen in the Greek (#281) means faithful, firm, verily, surely, truly, of a truth, and so be it or may it be fulfilled.

✝ Revelation 3:14, *"And unto the angel of the church of the Laodiceans write; These things saith the Amen, the faithful and true witness, the beginning of the creation of God;"*

BEGINNING AND THE END (Revelation 1:8; 21:6; 22:13)

> † Revelation 1:8, *"I am Alpha and Omega, the beginning and the ending, saith the Lord, which is, and which was, and which is to come, the Almighty."*
> † Revelation 21:6, *"And he said unto me, It is done. I am Alpha and Omega, the beginning and the end. I will give unto him that is athirst of the fountain of the water of life freely."*
> † Revelation 22:13, *"I am Alpha and Omega, the beginning and the end, the first and the last."*

BEGINNING OF THE CREATION OF GOD (Revelation 3:14)

> † Revelation 3:14, *"And unto the angel of the church of the Laodiceans write; These things saith the Amen, the faithful and true witness, the beginning of the creation of God;"*

FAITHFUL WITNESS (Revelation 1:5)
FIRST BEGOTTEN OF THE DEAD (Revelation 1:5)
PRINCE OF THE KINGS OF THE EARTH (Revelation 1:5)

> † Revelation 1:5, *"And from Jesus Christ, who is the faithful witness, and the first begotten of the dead, and the prince of the kings of the earth. Unto him that loved us, and washed us from our sins in his own blood,"*

FIRST AND THE LAST (Revelation 1:11, 17; 2:8; 22:13)

> † Revelation 1:11, *"Saying, I am Alpha and Omega, the first and the last: and, What thou seest, write in a book, and send it unto the seven churches which are in Asia; unto Ephesus, and unto Smyrna, and unto Pergamos, and unto Thyatira, and unto Sardis, and unto Philadelphia, and unto Laodicea."*
> † Revelation 1:17, *"And when I saw him, I fell at his feet as dead. And he laid his right hand upon me, saying unto me, Fear not; I am the first and the last:"*

† Revelation 2:8, *"And unto the angel of the church in Smyrna write; These things saith the first and the last, which was dead, and is alive;"*

† Revelation 22:13, *"I am Alpha and Omega, the beginning and the end, the first and the last."*

KING OF SAINTS (Revelation 15:3)

† Revelation 15:3, *"And they sing the song of Moses the servant of God, and the song of the Lamb, saying, Great and marvellous are thy works, Lord God Almighty; just and true are thy ways, thou King of saints."*

LAMB (Revelation 13:8)

† Revelation 13:8, *"And all that dwell upon the earth shall worship him, whose names are not written in the book of life of the Lamb slain from the foundation of the world."*

LION OF THE TRIBE OF JUDAH (Revelation 5:5)

† Revelation 5:5, *"And one of the elders saith unto me, Weep not: behold, the Lion of the tribe of Judah, the Root of David, hath prevailed to open the book, and to loose the seven seals thereof."*

BRIGHT AND MORNING STAR (Revelation 22:16)
ROOT AND THE OFFSPRING OF DAVID (Revelation 22:16)

† Revelation 22:16, *"I Jesus have sent mine angel to testify unto you these things in the churches. I am the root and the offspring of David, and the bright and morning star."*

WORD OF GOD (Revelation 19:13)

† Revelation 19:13, *"And he was clothed with a vesture dipped in blood: and his name is called The Word of God."*

NAMES FOR SATAN IN REVELATION

ABADDON – In the Greek Strong's Concordance (#3) a Hebrew name which means destruction or ruin. (Revelation 9:11)

APOLLYON – In the Greek (#623) means destroyer and angel of the bottomless pit. (Revelation 9:11)

    † Revelation 9:11, *"And they had a king over them, which is the angel of the bottomless pit, whose name in the Hebrew tongue is Abaddon, but in the Greek tongue hath his name Apollyon."*

ACCUSER OF THE BRETHREN (Revelation 12:10)

    † Revelation 12:10, *"And I heard a loud voice saying in heaven, Now is come salvation, and strength, and the kingdom of our God, and the power of his Christ: for the accuser of our brethren is cast down, which accused them before our God day and night."*

GREAT DRAGON (Revelation 12:9)
OLD SERPENT (Revelation 12:9)
DEVIL (Revelation 12:9)
SATAN (Revelation 12:9)

    † Revelation 12:9, *"And the great dragon was cast out, that old serpent, called the Devil, and Satan, which deceiveth the whole world: he was cast out into the earth, and his angels were cast out with him."*

LIST OF SEVENS IN REVELATION

SEVENS	REVELATION SCRIPTURES
Seven Angels	8:2, 6; 15:1, 6, 7, 8; 16:1; 17:1; 21:9 (Seven angels of the seven churches represents the leaders, pastors, or assigned angel over the church)
Seven Churches	1:4; 2-3
Seven Crowns	**2:10; 4:4, 10; 6:2; 9:7; 12:1; 14:14** (a set of seven scriptures refer to crown - "*stephanos*" in the Greek) (Three scriptures **12:3; 13:1; and 19:12** refer to crown - "*diadema*" in the Greek) "Seven crowns" is found in 12:3 Diadema- Strong's #1238- a blue band with white for Perisan Kings to bind on the turban – a kingly ornament Stephanos- Strong's #4735- a mark of royal or exalted rank, a wreath or garland used for victory in public games, a crown, a wreath
Seven Eyes	5:6
Seven Golden Lampstands/ Candlesticks	1:12, 20; 2:1; 4:5
Seven Heads	12:3; 13:1 (Seven heads are the seven mountains/hills which are the seven Kings/Kingdoms)
Seven Horns	5:6
Seven "I know thy works"	2: 2,9, 13, 19; 3:1, 8, 15
Seven Kings/Kingdoms	17:10, 11 (Assyria, Medo-Persia, Greece, Egypt, Babylon, Rome and the future kingdom thought to be a revived Roman Empire)
Seven Letters	2-3
Seven Mountains/Hills	17:9 (Mountains are a symbol of Kingdoms)
Seven Seals	5:1; 5:5
Seven Spirits	1:4; 3:1; 4:5; 5:6
Seven Stars	1:16, 20; 2:1; 3:1 (Seven stars are the seven angels of the seven churches)
Seven Torches, lamps of fire	4:5
Seven Thousand people	11:13
Seven Thunders	10:3, 4
Seven Trumpets	8:2, 6
Seven Plagues	15:1, 6, 8; 21:9
Seven Vials/Bowls	15:7; 16:1; 17:1; 21:9

REFERENCED SCRIPTURES

✝ Revelation 1:4, *"John to the seven churches which are in Asia: Grace be unto you, and peace, from him which is, and which was, and which is to come; and from the seven Spirits which are before his throne;"*

✝ Revelation 1:12, *"And I turned to see the voice that spake with me. And being turned, I saw seven golden candlesticks;"*

✝ Revelation 1:16, *"And he had in his right hand seven stars: and out of his mouth went a sharp two-edged sword: and his countenance was as the sun shineth in his strength."*

✝ Revelation 1:20, *"The mystery of the seven stars which thou sawest in my right hand, and the seven golden candlesticks. The seven stars are the angels of the seven churches: and the seven candlesticks which thou sawest are the seven churches."*

✝ Revelation 2:1, *"Unto the angel of the church of Ephesus write; These things saith he that holdeth the seven stars in his right hand, who walketh in the midst of the seven golden candlesticks;"*

✝ Revelation 2:2, *"I know thy works, and thy labour, and thy patience, and how thou canst not bear them which are evil: and thou hast tried them which say they are apostles, and are not, and hast found them liars:"*

✝ Revelation 2:9, *"I know thy works, and tribulation, and poverty, (but thou art rich) and I know the blasphemy of them which say they are Jews, and are not, but are the synagogue of Satan."*

✝ Revelation 2:10, *"Fear none of those things which thou shalt suffer: behold, the devil shall cast some of you into prison, that ye may be tried; and ye shall have tribulation ten days: be thou faithful unto death, and I will give thee a crown of life."*

✝ Revelation 2:13, *"I know thy works, and where thou dwellest, even where Satan's seat is: and thou holdest fast my name, and hast not denied my faith, even in those days wherein Antipas was my faithful martyr, who was slain among you, where Satan dwelleth."*

† Revelation 2:19, *"I know thy works, and charity, and service, and faith, and thy patience, and thy works; and the last to be more than the first."*

† Revelation 3:1, *"And unto the angel of the church in Sardis write; These things saith he that hath the seven Spirits of God, and the seven stars; I know thy works, that thou hast a name that thou livest, and art dead."*

† Revelation 3:8, *"I know thy works: behold, I have set before thee an open door, and no man can shut it: for thou hast a little strength, and hast kept my word, and hast not denied my name."*

† Revelation 3:15, *"I know thy works, that thou art neither cold nor hot: I would thou wert cold or hot."*

† Revelation 4:4, *"And round about the throne were four and twenty seats: and upon the seats I saw four and twenty elders sitting, clothed in white raiment; and they had on their heads crowns of gold."*

† Revelation 4:5, *"And out of the throne proceeded lightnings and thunderings and voices: and there were seven lamps of fire burning before the throne, which are the seven Spirits of God."*

† Revelation 4:10, *"The four and twenty elders fall down before him that sat on the throne, and worship him that liveth for ever and ever, and cast their crowns before the throne, saying,"*

† Revelation 5:1, *"And I saw in the right hand of him that sat on the throne a book written within and on the backside, sealed with seven seals."*

† Revelation 5:5, *"And one of the elders saith unto me, Weep not: behold, the Lion of the tribe of Juda, the Root of David, hath prevailed to open the book, and to loose the seven seals thereof."*

† Revelation 5:6, *"And I beheld, and, lo, in the midst of the throne and of the four beasts, and in the midst of the elders, stood a Lamb as it had been slain, having seven horns and seven eyes, which are the seven Spirits of God sent forth into all the earth."*

† Revelation 6:2, *"And I saw, and behold a white horse: and he that sat on him had a bow; and a crown was given unto him: and he went forth conquering, and to conquer."*

† Revelation 8:2, *"And I saw the seven angels which stood before God; and to them were given seven trumpets."*

† Revelation 8:6, *"And the seven angels which had the seven trumpets prepared themselves to sound."*

† Revelation 9:7, *"And the shapes of the locusts were like unto horses prepared unto battle; and on their heads were as it were crowns like gold, and their faces were as the faces of men."*

† Revelation 10:3, *"And cried with a loud voice, as when a lion roareth: and when he had cried, seven thunders uttered their voices."*

† Revelation 10:4, *"And when the seven thunders had uttered their voices, I was about to write: and I heard a voice from heaven saying unto me, Seal up those things which the seven thunders uttered, and write them not."*

† Revelation 11:13, *"And the same hour was there a great earthquake, and the tenth part of the city fell, and in the earthquake were slain of men seven thousand: and the remnant were affrighted, and gave glory to the God of heaven."*

† Revelation 12:1, *"And there appeared a great wonder in heaven; a woman clothed with the sun, and the moon under her feet, and upon her head a crown of twelve stars:"*

† Revelation 12:3, *"And there appeared another wonder in heaven; and behold a great red dragon, having seven heads and ten horns, and seven crowns upon his heads."*

† Revelation 13:1, *"And I stood upon the sand of the sea, and saw a beast rise up out of the sea, having seven heads and ten horns, and upon his horns ten crowns, and upon his heads the name of blasphemy."*

† Revelation 14:14, *"And I looked, and behold a white cloud, and upon the cloud one sat like unto the Son of man, having on his head a golden crown, and in his hand a sharp sickle."*

† Revelation 15:1, *"And I saw another sign in heaven, great and marvellous, seven angels having the seven last plagues; for in them is filled up the wrath of God."*

† Revelation 15:6, "And the seven angels came out of the temple, having the seven plagues, clothed in pure and white linen, and having their breasts girded with golden girdles."

† Revelation 15:7, "And one of the four beasts gave unto the seven angels seven golden vials full of the wrath of God, who liveth for ever and ever."

† Revelation 15:8, "And the temple was filled with smoke from the glory of God, and from his power; and no man was able to enter into the temple, till the seven plagues of the seven angels were fulfilled."

† Revelation 16:1, "And I heard a great voice out of the temple saying to the seven angels, Go your ways, and pour out the vials of the wrath of God upon the earth."

† Revelation 17:1, "And there came one of the seven angels which had the seven vials, and talked with me, saying unto me, Come hither; I will shew unto thee the judgment of the great whore that sitteth upon many waters:"

† Revelation 17:3, "So he carried me away in the spirit into the wilderness: and I saw a woman sit upon a scarlet coloured beast, full of names of blasphemy, having seven heads and ten horns."

† Revelation 17:7, "And the angel said unto me, Wherefore didst thou marvel? I will tell thee the mystery of the woman, and of the beast that carrieth her, which hath the seven heads and ten horns."

† Revelation 17:9, "And here is the mind which hath wisdom. The seven heads are seven mountains, on which the woman sitteth."

† Revelation 17:10, "And there are seven kings: five are fallen, and one is, and the other is not yet come; and when he cometh, he must continue a short space." Revelation 17:11, "And the beast that was, and is not, even he is the eighth, and is of the seven, and goeth into perdition."

† Revelation 19:12, "His eyes were as a flame of fire, and on his head were many crowns; and he had a name written, that no man knew, but he himself."

† Revelation 21:9, "And there came unto me one of the seven angels which had the seven vials full of the seven last plagues, and talked

with me, saying, Come hither, I will shew thee the bride, the Lamb's wife."

RECOMMENDED ACTIVITIES

1. Read Revelation again in another version. Make a list of questions as you read. Make a list of symbols, events, numbers, people and places that are not listed above.
2. As you read, try to identify areas of language, geographical, cultural and historical contexts. Apply some of the principles mentioned in this chapter.
3. Search other principles of interpretation on the Internet or using the book

Interpreting the Scriptures: A Textbook On How To Interpret The Bible written by Kevin J. Conner and Ken Malmin.

PERSONAL NOTES

CHAPTER THREE

'APOKALUPSIS'

The Book of Revelation describes visions experienced and given to Apostle John on the Isle of Patmos (Rev. 1:9-11). It describes the revelation of Jesus Christ and discloses His very essence: who He is and who He has always been. It explains His plan for the future in relationship to the church and to Israel. Notice it was a revelation, singular rather than plural. Therefore, the book is titled Revelation, not Revelations, as many erroneously pronounce. Just what does revelation mean? It comes from the Greek word *'apokalupsis'* (Strong's #602) meaning a disclosure of truth or instruction concerning things before unknown. It can mean laying bare, making naked, manifestation, and appearance. More suitable for our understanding it describes the uncovering, unveiling, and disclosing the person of Jesus Christ and His future plan of the church, the end times and eternal life. *'Apokalupsis'* is a noun used eighteen times in the New Testament but only once in the book of Revelation (1:1). It is translated as revelation, light, appearing, lighten, for the manifestation, and the coming.

(Luke 2:32 --lighten, Romans 2:5, Romans 8:19 --manifestation, Romans 16:25, First Corinthians 1:7 --for the coming, First Corinthians 14:6, First Corinthians 14:26, Second Corinthians 12:1, Second Corinthians 12:7, Galatians 1:12, Galatians 2:2, Ephesians 1:17, Ephesians 3:3, Second

Thessalonians 1:7, First Peter 1:7 -- appearing, First Peter 1:13, First Peter 4:13 --revealed, Revelation 1:1).

The Book of Daniel, in the Old Testament, is another apocalyptic book and should be studied alongside of the Book of Revelation. Daniel and Revelation often parallel. For example, compare Daniel 12:7 to Revelation 11: 9, 11; Daniel 7:4-6 and Revelation 13:2.

† Daniel 7:4-6, *"The first was like a lion, and had eagle's wings: I beheld till the wings thereof were plucked, and it was lifted up from the earth, and made stand upon the feet as a man, and a man's heart was given to it. ⁵And behold another beast, a second, like to a bear, and it raised up itself on one side, and it had three ribs in the mouth of it between the teeth of it: and they said thus unto it, Arise, devour much flesh. ⁶After this I beheld, and lo another, like a leopard, which had upon the back of it four wings of a fowl; the beast had also four heads; and dominion was given to it."*

† Daniel 12:7, *"And I heard the man clothed in linen, which was upon the waters of the river, when he held up his right hand and his left hand unto heaven, and sware by him that liveth for ever that it shall be for a time, times, and an half; and when he shall have accomplished to scatter the power of the holy people, all these things shall be finished."*

† Revelation 11:9, *"And they of the people and kindreds and tongues and nations shall see their dead bodies three days and an half, and shall not suffer their dead bodies to be put in graves."*

† Revelation 11:11, *"And after three days and an half the Spirit of life from God entered into them, and they stood upon their feet; and great fear fell upon them which saw them."*

† Revelation 13:2, *"And the beast which I saw was like unto a leopard, and his feet were as the feet of a bear, and his mouth as the mouth of a lion: and the dragon gave him his power, and his seat, and great authority."*

The theological study of the end times dealing with death and eternal future of the soul is called eschatology. Eschatology is the study of what the Bible says will happen in the end. God did not want us to be ignorant of His person and His plan (Romans 11:25; First Corinthians 10:1,15:34; Hebrews 5:2). A long time ago God gave us the knowledge we would need through the Bible writers, the inspired Word of God. John wrote Revelation near the end of the first century, probably around 96 AD but it may be dated as early as 68-69 AD. Daniel wrote the Book of Daniel as evidenced by Daniel 9:2 and 10:2 when he refers to himself as I, Daniel. In Matthew 24:15, Jesus confirms Daniel as the author. Daniel was most likely written around 540 BC.

REFERENCED SCRIPTURES

+ Daniel 9:2, *"In the first year of his reign I Daniel understood by books the number of the years, whereof the word of the* Lord *came to Jeremiah the prophet, that he would accomplish seventy years in the desolations of Jerusalem."*
+ Daniel 10:2, *"In those days I Daniel was mourning three full weeks."*
+ Matthew 24:15, *"When ye therefore shall see the abomination of desolation, spoken of by Daniel the prophet, stand in the holy place, (whoso readeth, let him understand:)"*
+ Luke 2:32, *"A light to lighten the Gentiles, and the glory of thy people Israel."*
+ Romans 2:5, *"But after thy hardness and impenitent heart treasurest up unto thyself wrath against the day of wrath and revelation of the righteous judgment of God;"*
+ Romans 8:19, *"For the earnest expectation of the creature waiteth for the manifestation of the sons of God."*
+ Romans 11:25, *"For I would not, brethren, that ye should be ignorant of this mystery, lest ye should be wise in your own conceits; that blindness in part is happened to Israel, until the fulness of the Gentiles be come in."*
+ Romans 16:25, *"Now to him that is of power to stablish you according to my gospel, and the preaching of Jesus Christ, according to the revelation of the mystery, which was kept secret since the world began,"*
+ First Corinthians 1:7, *"So that ye come behind in no gift; waiting for the coming of our Lord Jesus Christ"*

† First Corinthians 10:1, *"Moreover, brethren, I would not that ye should be ignorant, how that all our fathers were under the cloud, and all passed through the sea;"*

† First Corinthians 14:6, *"Now, brethren, if I come unto you speaking with tongues, what shall I profit you, except I shall speak to you either by revelation, or by knowledge, or by prophesying, or by doctrine?"*

† First Corinthians 14:26, *"How is it then, brethren? when ye come together, every one of you hath a psalm, hath a doctrine, hath a tongue, hath a revelation, hath an interpretation. Let all things be done unto edifying."*

† First Corinthians 15:34, *"Awake to righteousness, and sin not; for some have not the knowledge of God: I speak this to your shame."*

† Second Corinthians 12:1, *"It is not expedient for me doubtless to glory. I will come to visions and revelations of the Lord."*

† Second Corinthians 12:7, *"And lest I should be exalted above measure through the abundance of the revelations, there was given to me a thorn in the flesh, the messenger of Satan to buffet me, lest I should be exalted above measure."*

† Galatians 1:12, *"For I neither received it of man, neither was I taught it, but by the revelation of Jesus Christ."*

† Galatians 2:2, *"And I went up by revelation, and communicated unto them that gospel which I preach among the Gentiles, but privately to them which were of reputation, lest by any means I should run, or had run, in vain."*

† Ephesians 1:17, *"That the God of our Lord Jesus Christ, the Father of glory, may give unto you the spirit of wisdom and revelation in the knowledge of him:"*

† Ephesians 3:3, *"How that by revelation he made known unto me the mystery; (as I wrote afore in few words,"*

† Second Thessalonians 1:7, *"And to you who are troubled rest with us, when the Lord Jesus shall be revealed from heaven with his mighty angels,"*

† Hebrews 5:2, *"Who can have compassion on the ignorant, and on them that are out of the way; for that he himself also is compassed with infirmity."*

† First Peter 1:7, *"That the trial of your faith, being much more precious than of gold that perisheth, though it be tried with fire, might be found unto praise and honour and glory at the appearing of Jesus Christ:"*

† First Peter 1:13, *"Wherefore gird up the loins of your mind, be sober, and hope to the end for the grace that is to be brought unto you at the revelation of Jesus Christ;"*

† First Peter 4:13, *"But rejoice, inasmuch as ye are partakers of Christ's sufferings; that, when his glory shall be revealed, ye may be glad also with exceeding joy."*

† Revelation 1:1, *"The Revelation of Jesus Christ, which God gave unto him, to shew unto his servants things which must shortly come to pass; and he sent and signified it by his angel unto his servant John:"*

† Revelation 1:9-11, *"⁹I John, who also am your brother, and companion in tribulation, and in the kingdom and patience of Jesus Christ, was in the isle that is called Patmos, for the word of God, and for the testimony of Jesus Christ. ¹⁰I was in the Spirit on the Lord's day, and heard behind me a great voice, as of a trumpet, ¹¹Saying, I am Alpha and Omega, the first and the last: and, What thou seest, write in a book, and send it unto the seven churches which are in Asia; unto Ephesus, and unto Smyrna, and unto Pergamos, and unto Thyatira,* and unto Sardis, and unto Philadelphia, and unto Laodicea."

RECOMMENDED ACTIVITIES

1. Read the Book of Daniel in different versions.
2. Find the word 'revelation' in the Greek #602 in a Strong's Exhaustive Concordance. You may also find it on the Internet using sources like:
   https://biblehub.com/
   https://www.biblegateway.com/
   https://www.biblestudytools.com/
   https://www.studylight.org
3. Identify the revelation of Jesus Christ as you study each chapter of Revelation.

CHAPTER FOUR

VARIOUS VIEWS

There are various views of the events of end time prophecy. This writing will present the **Pre-Tribulation Rapture and a Premillennial Second Coming of Christ** view with appropriate explanations in the following chapters. The following views are the most commonly deliberated but as you read other materials you will find multiple considerations of the end time events. It is important that you be sure the material you study correlates to the Word of God. That is why I thought it so important to back up this writing with the scriptures written directly into the text.

CONCERNING THE TIMING OF THE RAPTURE WITH TIMING OF THE TRIBULATION PERIOD

- **A Pre-Tribulation Rapture suggests that the Rapture of the church will occur before the Tribulation Period.**
- A Mid-Tribulation Rapture anticipates the Rapture in the middle of the Tribulation.
- A Post-Tribulation Rapture expects the Rapture at the end of the Tribulation period and before the second coming of Jesus.

Pre-Tribulation Rapture

> Church Age---**Rapture**---Tribulation---Second Coming---Millennium---
> Great White Throne Judgment---New Heaven and New Earth (Eternity)

Mid-Tribulation Rapture

> Church Age---First Half of Tribulation---**Rapture**--- Second Half
> of Tribulation---Second Coming---Millennium---Great White
> Throne Judgment---New Heaven and New Earth (Eternity)

Post-Tribulation Rapture

> Church Age--Tribulation---**Rapture and Second Coming**---Millennium---
> Great White Throne Judgment---New Heaven and New Earth (Eternity)

CONCERNING THE TIMING OF THE SECOND COMING OF CHRIST IN RELATION TO THE MILLENNIUM

Millennialism refers to the beliefs in the thousand-year reign of Christ (Revelation 20).

1. **A Dispensational Premillennial view believes the Second Coming of Christ will occur before the 1000-year reign of Christ (Millennium).** ***There is another view called Historic Premillennialism. That one we are not dealing with here. That view holds that the church has replaced the nation of Israel as God's chosen people. The Dispensational Premillennial view, which we are discussing holds that God will still give Israel the land promised in Genesis 15:18.

† Genesis 15:18, "In the same day the LORD made a covenant with Abram, saying, Unto thy seed have I given this land, from the river of Egypt unto the great river, the river Euphrates:"

2. A Postmillennial belief that the Second Coming of Christ occurs after the Millennium.

3. An Amillennial view refers to the absence of an earthly millennial reign. They believe the reign of Christ is in your heart and upon the Second Coming Christ will resurrect the dead and judge them. In other words, the Second Coming and the resurrection of saved and unsaved occur simultaneously.

Premillennial Second Coming

Church Age---Rapture---Tribulation---**Second Coming---Millennium---** Great White Throne Judgment---New Heaven and New Earth (Eternity)

Post Millennial Second Coming

Church Age---Tribulation---**Millennium---Second Coming---**Great White Throne Judgment---New Heaven and New Earth (Eternity)

Amillennial Second Coming

Church Age---**Second Coming---**Great White Throne Judgment---New Heaven and New Earth (Eternity)

RECOMMENDED ACTIVITIES

1. Look up these words on a reputable site on the Internet: Pre-Tribulation and Premillennial. Rose Book of Bible Charts & Timelines is an excellent source to study the various views.
2. Compare these to the other views mentioned above.

PERSONAL NOTES

CHAPTER FIVE

THE CHURCH AGE

All over the world, Jesus Christ has been building His church for over 2000 years. Matthew 16:18 reads, "And I say also unto thee, That thou art Peter, and upon this rock I will build my church; and the gates of hell shall not prevail against it." We currently live in a time called the Church Age. The Church Age began with the birth of the Church in Acts 2 on the day of Pentecost. The Church Age will end on the day of the Rapture. This time is called "Fullness of the Gentiles" in Romans 11:25. Don't confuse this with the "Time of the Gentiles" which began with King Nebuchadnezzar and the Babylonian Captivity and will end with the Second Coming (Daniel 2; Luke 21:24). This speaks to the Gentile political dominion until the Second Coming. Daniel's vision of Nebuchadnezzar in Daniel 2 included metaphors of gold, silver, bronze, iron, and clay. These images represented Gentile nations that would govern the world until Jesus returns to rule in His Kingdom. This is the time between the 69 and 70 weeks that Daniel spoke about and will be discussed more later on.

† Luke 21:24, "And they shall fall by the edge of the sword, and shall be led away captive into all nations: and Jerusalem shall

be trodden down of the Gentiles, until the times of the Gentiles be fulfilled."

✝ Romans 11:25, "For I would not, brethren, that ye should be ignorant of this mystery, lest ye should be wise in your own conceits; that blindness in part is happened to Israel, until the fulness of the Gentiles be come in."

In Revelation chapters two and three, John references seven churches. Each church represents a historical time period of the church. The church of Ephesus was the first church and historical representation. Laodicea is the last. We are currently in the last church age in history. Revelation chapters 2-3 are letters written by John appealing to the seven churches: Ephesus, Smyrna, Pergamos, Thyatira, Sardis, Philadelphia, and Laodicea. These letters no doubt circulated among all the churches. John told us the strengths and rebukes of each church. He encouraged them to repent and told of their consequence if they did not. John presented them the promise of God if they would heed the Word of the Lord. The chart on the next page summarizes and outlines the characteristics of each church.

Each of the seven churches may characterize the following:

1. Each church may exemplify the individual person as a type of the church. You are the temple of Christ. You are the church.
2. Each church may imply your local church.
3. Each church may symbolize the church as a body of Christ.
4. Each church represents a particular time or age in history.

We are living in the last historical church, the Church of Laodicea. Seven times the Book of Revelation says, "He that hath an ear, let him hear what the Spirit saith unto the churches;" (Revelation 2:7,11,17, 29; 3:6,13, 22). Yet, following a discourse on the Antichrist, Revelation 13:9 reads, "⁹ If any man have an ear, let him hear." The words *church and spirit* have been omitted. The church is never mentioned again after John writes his letter to Laodicea. When the Church Age ends, at the end of the Laodicean Church period, the Rapture will begin. See the chart on CHURCHES IN REVELATION.

CHURCHES IN REVELATION

CHURCH	EPHESUS Loveless Church	SMYRNA Suffering Church	PERGAMUM (PERGAMOS) Worldly Inner City Church
SCRIPTURE	Rev. 2:1-7	Rev. 2:8-11	Rev. 2:12-17
MEANING OF NAME	Permitted To let go Relax	Myrrh Anointing oil	Height or Elevation Married to power
COMMENDATION	Hard work Patient endurance Perseverance Rejects evil Hates deeds of Nicolaitans	Endures suffering and tribulation Poverty Yet it is rich	Loyalty to Christ Has not denied the faith Refuses to deny Him
CONDEMNATION	Left their first love	NONE	Holds doctrine of Baalam and Nicolaitans Tolerates cults, idolatry and immorality
ENCOURAGEMENT	Repent and do works as they did at first	Remain faithful unto death Fear not	Repent
ALTERNATIVE	He will come quickly Will remove candlestick out of his place (1:20)	NONE	He will come quickly And fight against them with sword of His mouth
REWARD	Will eat of the Tree of Life	Will receive the crown of Life They will not experience the 2nd death	Will eat of the hidden manna Receive a white stone with a new name written on it
CHRIST DEPICTION	Holds 7 stars in His right hand in the midst of 7 candlesticks (1:20)	First and Last Who was dead and is alive	Has the sharp sword with two edges (Hebrews 4:12)
HISTORICAL PERIOD REPRESENTED APPROXIMATE DATES (A.D.)	First century Church 33-100	The Persecuted Church of the 2nd and 3rd centuries 100-313	Church from about 312 -538 (Constantine)

THYATIRA Wrong Doctrine Church	SARDIS Spiritually Dead Church	PHILADELPHIA Spiritually Alive Church	LAODICEA Lukewarm Church
Rev. 2:18-29	Rev. 3:1-6	Rev. 3:7-13	Rev. 3:14-22
Odor of affliction Ruled by a woman	Red ones Precious stone	Brotherly love	Justice of the people Laity
Works (deeds) Love Faith Service Constant improvement	Works Name of being alive Some have not defiled their garments	Kept His word Has not denied His name	NONE
Tolerates cults, idolatry and immorality Tolerated false prophet Jezebel	Works not perfect before the Lord Dead church	NONE	Neither hot nor cold Lukewarm Doesn't realize wretched condition Poor and naked
Repent Hold fast which they already have till He comes	Be alert Wake up Strengthen what remains Repent Turn to Jesus again	Placed before them an open door Hold fast that no man take thy crown	Repent Turn from apathy Be zealous Buy (from Jesus) gold tried in fire clothes of white raiment Anoint eyes - salve
Great tribulation Children will be killed	He will come on them as a thief	So no man can take their crown	He will spew them out of His mouth
Will give power – authority over the nations Will receive gift of the Morning Star	Name will not be blotted out of the Book of Life Jesus will confess his name before the Father	Will keep them from the hour of temptation-trial Be made a pillar in the Temple of God in New Jerusalem	Those who overcome will sit with Him on His throne Fellowship with Christ Will sup with Him
Eyes like flames of fires Feet like fine brass	Has 7 spirits and 7 stars	True has the key of David	The Amen The faithful and true witness The beginning (originating) source of creation
Church of the Dark Ages till the 16th century 538-1517	Church of Renaissance and the Reformation period 1517-1844	Church of the Revival of the 19th century Modern Age of Mission 1755-1844	End times Last church NOW! 1844- present

SIGNS OF THE TIMES

The Bible tells us of the signs of the end. The signs of the times are evident today and corroborate that we are in the last days.

What are the signs of the times? The disciples asked Jesus the same thing concerning what were the signs of His coming (Matthew 24:3). As I write this book, many signs of the times are clearly discernable. I began writing many months ago but currently we are in the middle of the coronavirus (COVID-19) worldwide pandemic. The case is being made for global digital identification. Economic systems are on the brink of failure. People across the world are suffering from famine and this virus threatens even worsening conditions. Earthquakes and disasters are occurring more frequent. Iran is constantly threatening war. America is on the verge of becoming a socialist nation. Who would have ever imagined? Some countries in Africa are experiencing locust plagues. There are so many signs happening now that they cannot all be listed in this work. Matthew 24 and Luke 21 list numerous end time signs but the Bible documents several others. Some of the Biblical references to the signs of the times are written below followed by a summary of the signs described in that set of Scripture.

† Matthew 24:3, *"And as he sat upon the mount of Olives, the disciples came unto him privately, saying, Tell us, when shall these things be? and what shall be the sign of thy coming, and of the end of the world?"*

† Matthew 24: 5-12, *"⁵ For many shall come in my name, saying, I am Christ; and shall deceive many. ⁶And ye shall hear of wars and rumours of wars: see that ye be not troubled: for all these things must come to pass, but the end is not yet. ⁷For nation shall rise against nation, and kingdom against kingdom: and there shall be famines, and pestilences, and earthquakes, in divers places. ⁸All these are the beginning of sorrows. ⁹Then shall they deliver you up to be afflicted, and shall kill you: and ye shall be hated of all nations for my name's sake. ¹⁰And then shall many be offended, and shall betray one another, and shall hate one another. ¹¹And many false prophets shall rise, and*

shall deceive many.[12] And because iniquity shall abound, the love of many shall wax cold."

† Matthew 24:24, *"For there shall arise false Christs, and false prophets, and shall shew great signs and wonders; insomuch that, if it were possible, they shall deceive the very elect."*

† Matthew 24:33, *"So likewise ye, when ye shall see all these things, know that it is near, even at the doors."*

† Luke 21:7-12, *"[7]And they asked him, saying, Master, but when shall these things be? and what sign will there be when these things shall come to pass? [8]And he said, Take heed that ye be not deceived: for many shall come in my name, saying, I am Christ; and the time draweth near: go ye not therefore after them. [9]But when ye shall hear of wars and commotions, be not terrified: for these things must first come to pass; but the end is not by and by. [10]Then said he unto them, Nation shall rise against nation, and kingdom against kingdom: [11]And great earthquakes shall be in divers places, and famines, and pestilences; and fearful sights and great signs shall there be from heaven. [12]But before all these, they shall lay their hands on you, and persecute you, delivering you up to the synagogues, and into prisons, being brought before kings and rulers for my name's sake."*

† Luke 21:16-17, *"[16]And ye shall be betrayed both by parents, and brethren, and kinsfolks, and friends; and some of you shall they cause to be put to death. [17]And ye shall be hated of all men for my name's sake."*

SUMMARY

- Deceivers (lead away from the truth-- to lead astray)
- Wars and rumors of war, commotions
- Nation will rise against nation, kingdom against kingdom
- Famines
- Pestilences
- Earthquakes in divers places
- Affliction (pressure, stress, oppression)

- Kill (destroy, extinguish, abolish, perish, inflict mortal death)
- Hatred
- Offended
- Betray one another
- False prophets deceive
- Sin will abound
- Love of many will wax cold
- False Christs, False prophets who show signs and wonders
- Fearful signs and great signs from heaven
- Persecution of believers
- Imprisonment of believers
- Believers will be betrayed by family and friends and hated for the sake of the Lord

† Second Peter 2:1-3, *"¹But there were also false prophets among the people, just as there will be false teachers among you. They will secretly introduce destructive heresies, even denying the sovereign Lord who bought them—bringing swift destruction on themselves. ²Many will follow their depraved conduct and will bring the way of truth into disrepute. ³In their greed these teachers will exploit you with fabricated stories. Their condemnation has long been hanging over them, and their destruction has not been sleeping."*

SUMMARY

- False Prophets
- False teachers
- Destructive heresies
- Denying the Lord
- Many follow their depraved conduct
- Many will bring the way of truth into dispute
- Greed
- Exploitation with lies

† Second Peter 3:3-4, *"³Knowing this first, that there shall come in the last days scoffers, walking after their own lusts, ⁴And saying, Where is the promise of his coming? for since the fathers fell asleep, all things continue as they were from the beginning of the creation."*

SUMMARY

- Scoffer (mocker)
- Walking after their own lusts (desires, longing for what is forbidden)

† First Timothy 4:1-3, *"¹Now the Spirit speaketh expressly, that in the latter times some shall depart from the faith, giving heed to seducing spirits, and doctrines of devils; ²Speaking lies in hypocrisy; having their conscience seared with a hot iron; ³Forbidding to marry, and commanding to abstain from meats, which God hath created to be received with thanksgiving of them which believe and know the truth."*

SUMMARY

- Departure from the faith
- Gives heed to seducing spirits (wandering, roving, corrupter, misleading, imposters)
- Lies
- Hypocrisy
- Conscience seared with hot iron (no regard for what they say or do)
- Hypocrisy of those who forbid marriage
- Hypocrisy to abstain from meats (pretense of holiness)

† Second Timothy 3:1-8, *"¹This know also, that in the last days perilous times shall come. ²For men shall be lovers of their own selves, covetous, boasters, proud, blasphemers, disobedient to parents,*

unthankful, unholy, ³Without natural affection, trucebreakers, false accusers, incontinent, fierce, despisers of those that are good, ⁴Traitors, heady, high minded, lovers of pleasures more than lovers of God; ⁵Having a form of godliness, but denying the power thereof: from such turn away. ⁶For of this sort are they which creep into houses, and lead captive silly women laden with sins, led away with divers lusts, ⁷Ever learning, and never able to come to the knowledge of the truth. ⁸Now as Jannes and Jambres withstood Moses, so do these also resist the truth: men of corrupt minds, reprobate concerning the faith."

SUMMARY

- Lovers of themselves
- Covetous
- Boastful
- Proud
- Blasphemers
- Disobedient to their parents
- Unthankful
- Unholy
- Without natural affection
- Trucebreakers
- False accusers
- Incontinent (Without self-control)
- Fierce (Not tame)
- Despisers of those that are good
- Traitors
- Heady (Rash)
- High minded (Conceited, Proud)
- Lovers of pleasure rather than lovers of God
- Creep into homes and gain control over gullible women
- Have a form of righteousness but deny its power
- Led away with divers lusts (Loaded down with sins and swayed by all kinds of evil desires)

- Increased knowledge but not of the truth
- Resists the truth
- Corrupt minds
- Reprobate concerning the faith (Not standing the test, Unfit)

RECOMMENDED ACTIVITIES

1. Read Revelation chapters 2 and 3.
2. How do you understand the words, "He that hath an ear, let him hear what the Spirit saith unto the churches;" in Revelation 2:7, 11, 17, 29; 3:6,13, 22? (Hint: listen, pay attention).
3. Study the chart of the seven churches.
4. Which church best describes your individual relationship with God right now? What can you do to advance your relationship with God?
5. Which church best describes your local church? How can she improve? What can you do to facilitate a change?
6. Which church best represents the body of Christ as a whole? How do you see your role to bring about transformation?
7. Search the scriptures for more signs of end times. List as many as you can. Consider the Old Testament scriptures like Joel and Zechariah and parables of Jesus like Matthew 13: 24-52.

PERSONAL NOTES

CHAPTER SIX

THE RAPTURE

The Rapture begins when the Church Age ends. *Hereafter* in Revelation 4:1 is also translated as "after this", "what happens next", and "what takes place after this". *After this* refers to after the Church Age.

At the time of the Rapture, Daniel 9:27 tells us the Antichrist will sign a Treaty with Israel for one week. The signing of the treaty signals the beginning of the Tribulation. The treaty signing happens at or near the time of the Rapture and before the Tribulation. One week is seven years. However, in the middle of the week, which is three- and one-half years, the Antichrist will break the treaty (Daniel 9:27).

† Revelation 4:1, *"After this I looked, and, behold, a door was opened in heaven: and the first voice which I heard was as it were of a trumpet talking with me; which said, Come up hither, and I will shew thee things which must be hereafter."*

† Daniel 9:27, *"And he shall confirm the covenant with many for one week: and in the midst of the week he shall cause the sacrifice and the oblation to cease, and for the overspreading of abominations he shall make it desolate, even until the consummation, and that determined shall be poured upon the desolate."*

As long as the Church remains on earth, the larger part of Revelation fulfillment cannot take place. When Jesus comes in the Rapture, the Church (New Testament saints) will be caught up and will meet Him in the air. Apostle Paul wrote in First Thessalonians 4:16:

> † First Thessalonians 4:16, *"For the Lord himself shall descend from heaven with a shout, with the voice of the archangel, and with the trump of God: and the dead in Christ shall rise first:"*

This means that the Church, those who repented and followed Christ, will rise from their graves and will be caught up in the clouds. Those who rejected Christ will be left behind. Old Testament saints and the Tribulation saints will be resurrected after the tribulation. Chapter seven is devoted to resurrections in more detail.

No one except the Father knows the time and day but believers are absolutely not ignorant concerning the times and seasons.

> † Matthew 24:36, *"But of that day and hour knoweth no man, no, not the angels of heaven, but my Father only."*

First Thessalonians 5:1-2 confirms that believers know the times and seasons.

Believers being full of the Holy Spirit know the time is near.

> † First Thessalonians 5:1-2, *"But of the times and the seasons, brethren, ye have no need that I write unto you. ² For yourselves know perfectly that the day of the Lord so cometh as a thief in the night."*

Prophecies have been fulfilled and we are now living in the period of the Laodicean Church, the last church age before the Rapture. The word Rapture does not appear in the Bible. It comes from a Latin word *rapare* meaning to seize. Nonetheless the Bible unquestionably speaks to it. The Greek word for "caught up" is "harpazo" (#726 in the Strong's Concordance). It means to snatch out or snatch away, to carry off.

† First Thessalonians 4:17, *"Then we which are alive and remain shall be caught up together with them in the clouds, to meet the Lord in the air: and so shall we ever be with the Lord."*

Some question the idea of a Pre-Tribulation Rapture (where the Rapture occurs before the Tribulation). However, the Bible never says the Church will go through the Tribulation.

God does not destine us to wrath as written in:

† First Thessalonians 5:9, *"For God hath not appointed us to wrath, but to obtain salvation by our Lord Jesus Christ,"*

The Lord has promised to keep us from the hour of trial or temptation.

† Revelation 3:10, *"Because thou hast kept the word of my patience, I also will keep thee from the hour of temptation, which shall come upon all the world, to try them that dwell upon the earth."*

The Church will accompany Christ when He comes at the Second Coming after the tribulation. We read in:

† First Thessalonians 3:13, *"To the end he may stablish your hearts unblameable in holiness before God, even our Father, at the coming of our Lord Jesus Christ with all his saints."*

Shadrach, Meshach, and Abednego, in the book of Daniel, are believed by many scholars to imply the Jews during the Tribulation. We notice Daniel's absence from the fiery furnace. Many scholars believe his absence prefigures the Church being absent from the Tribulation. This would support Pre-Tribulation Rapture.

† Daniel 3: 23-25, *"²³ And these three men, Shadrach, Meshach, and Abednego, fell down bound into the midst of the burning fiery furnace.²⁴ Then Nebuchadnezzar the king was astonished, and rose up in haste, and spake, and said unto his counsellors, Did not we cast*

three men bound into the midst of the fire? They answered and said unto the king, True, O king.²⁵ He answered and said, Lo, I see four men loose, walking in the midst of the fire, and they have no hurt; and the form of the fourth is like the Son of God."

Furthermore, the Church will be married to Jesus at the Marriage of the Lamb in heaven. This event happens sometime before the Second Coming and probably after the Judgment Seat of Christ. The Marriage Supper of the Lamb event, different than the Marriage of the Lamb, takes place on earth sometime at the Second Coming of Christ.

✝ Revelation 19:7-9, *"⁷Let us be glad and rejoice, and give honour to him: for the marriage of the Lamb is come, and his wife hath made herself ready. ⁸ And to her was granted that she should be arrayed in fine linen, clean and white: for the fine linen is the righteousness of saints. ⁹And he saith unto me, Write, Blessed are they which are called unto the marriage supper of the Lamb. And he saith unto me, These are the true sayings of God."*

Wedding customs in the time of Christ were different than our present western customs. There were at least three phases to the marriage. After the marriage contract was signed by each of the parents, the betrothal period or engagement began. It lasted about a year. Secondly, just like in the parable of the ten virgins in Matthew 25:1-13, the bridegroom and his male friends go to the house of the bride at midnight. They all joined up and paraded down the streets and ended up at the home of the bride. Thirdly, there was a marriage supper like the one at the wedding of Cana in John 2:1-2. After the Church gets raptured, she will participate in various events such as this in heaven as those left on earth go through the Tribulation. These events will be discussed in the chapter devoted solely to the Tribulation.

PERSONAL NOTES

CHAPTER SEVEN

CONCERNING DEATHS AND RESURRECTIONS

From the moment we are born we begin to die. We will all die. Some will die once while others die twice. The study of end times deals much with first and second deaths, as well as, the resurrection of different groups. Some explanations are necessary to clarify what is meant by deaths and resurrections. Let's first consider deaths since there must be a death before there can be a resurrection.

† Hebrews 9:27, *"And as it is appointed unto men once to die, but after this the judgment:"*

All people will have a "first death" but all people will not have a second death. Both saints and sinners will die a "first death" but only sinners will die a "second death". The second death has no power over believers. The believer will be given eternal life and will die the natural death but not a spiritual death.

✝ "Revelation 20:6, *"Blessed and holy is he that hath part in the first resurrection: on such the second death hath no power, but they shall be priests of God and of Christ, and shall reign with him a thousand years."*

"Second death" applies to those who do not believe in Jesus Christ and have not repented of their sins. Sinners will die a first death or a natural death but will also die a spiritual and eternal death. This death refers to being totally cut off physically and spiritually from God forevermore. Those who die a second death will lose the opportunity to ever again accept Jesus, as Lord. They will spend their eternal life in hell in a literal burning fire without even one drop of water to quench thirst.

The second death is mentioned four times in Scripture.

✝ Revelation 2:11, *"He that hath an ear, let him hear what the Spirit saith unto the churches; He that overcometh shall not be hurt of the second death."*

✝ Revelation 20:6, *"Blessed and holy is he that hath part in the first resurrection: on such the second death hath no power, but they shall be priests of God and of Christ, and shall reign with him a thousand years."*

✝ Revelation 20:14, *"And death and hell were cast into the lake of fire. This is the second death."*

✝ Revelation 21:8, *"But the fearful, and unbelieving, and the abominable, and murderers, and whoremongers, and sorcerers, and idolaters, and all liars, shall have their part in the lake which burneth with fire and brimstone: which is the second death."*

FIRST DEATH	SECOND DEATH
Natural physical death	Eternal death
All will die this death	Only sinners will experience
	Separation from God forever

We will all die a natural death and we will all be resurrected from the natural death. The difference will be the timing of the resurrection and the place of eternal destiny.

The Bible talks of two resurrections: the first and second resurrection. These two resurrections are for two different groups of people; the saved and the non-saved.

FIRST RESURRECTION SAVED (JUST)	SECOND RESURRECTION UNSAVED (UNJUST)

† Isaiah 26:19, *"Thy dead men shall live, together with my dead body shall they arise. Awake and sing, ye that dwell in dust: for thy dew is as the dew of herbs, and the earth shall cast out the dead."*

† Luke 14:14, *"And thou shalt be blessed; for they cannot recompense thee: for thou shalt be recompensed at the resurrection of the just."*

† John 5: 28-29, *"28Marvel not at this: for the hour is coming, in the which all that are in the graves shall hear his voice, 29And shall come forth; they that have done good, unto the resurrection of life; and they that have done evil, unto the resurrection of damnation."*

† Acts 24:15, *"And have hope toward God, which they themselves also allow, that there shall be a resurrection of the dead, both of the just and unjust."*

† Daniel 12:1-2, *"1And at that time shall Michael stand up, the great prince which standeth for the children of thy people: and there shall be a time of trouble, such as never was since there was a nation even to that same time: and at that time thy people shall be delivered, every one that shall be found written in the book. 2And many of them that sleep in the dust of the earth shall awake, some to everlasting life, and some to shame and everlasting contempt."*

When believers die, their souls depart to heaven but their bodies remain in the grave until they are resurrected. This will be discussed in detail.

When non-believers die, their souls go to hell and will eventually be cast into the eternal lake of fire. Their bodies remain in the grave until after the millennium at the time of the Great White Throne Judgment.

Resurrection refers to when the bodies will be raised from the dead. The bodies of all believers and all non-believers will be resurrected from the dead but will resurrect at different times and go to different places.

- † Second Corinthians 5:8, *"We are confident, I say, and willing rather to be absent from the body, and to be present with the Lord."*
- † Revelation 20:13-15, *"¹³And the sea gave up the dead which were in it; and death and hell delivered up the dead which were in them: and they were judged every man according to their works. ¹⁴And death and hell were cast into the lake of fire. This is the second death. ¹⁵And whosoever was not found written in the book of life was cast into the lake of fire."*
- † John 5:28-29, *"²⁸Marvel not at this: for the hour is coming, in the which all that are in the graves shall hear his voice, ²⁹And shall come forth; they that have done good, unto the resurrection of life; and they that have done evil, unto the resurrection of damnation."*

The resurrection of the saints or the first resurrection refers to when our mortal bodies resurrect from the dead to be joined with our spirit and be clothed with an immortal body. This is called our glorified bodies. Our bodies will be like Jesus' glorified body.

- † First Corinthians 15:42-53, *"⁴²So also is the resurrection of the dead. It is sown in corruption; it is raised in incorruption: ⁴³It is sown in dishonour; it is raised in glory: it is sown in weakness; it is raised in power: ⁴⁴It is sown a natural body; it is raised a spiritual body. There is a natural body, and there is a spiritual body. ⁴⁵And so it is written, The first man Adam was made a living soul; the last Adam was made a quickening spirit. ⁴⁶Howbeit that was not first which is spiritual, but that which is natural; and afterward that which is* *spiritual. ⁴⁷The first man is of the earth, earthy; the second man is the Lord from heaven. ⁴⁸As is the earthy, such are they also that are earthy: and as is the heavenly, such are they also that are heavenly. ⁴⁹And as we have borne the image of the earthy, we shall also bear the image of the heavenly. ⁵⁰Now this I say, brethren, that flesh and blood cannot inherit the kingdom of God; neither doth corruption inherit incorruption. ⁵¹Behold, I shew you a mystery; We shall not all sleep, but we shall all be changed, ⁵²In a moment, in the twinkling of an eye, at the last trump: for the trumpet shall sound, and the dead shall be raised incorruptible, and we shall be changed. ⁵³For this corruptible must put on incorruption, and this mortal must put on immortality."*

The first resurrection takes place in various stages and at various times. The chart following this discussion will help to illustrate.

First: The resurrection of Jesus and some Old Testament Jerusalem saints. It is amazing how the resurrected bodies appeared unto many! This resurrection has already happened.

✝ First Corinthians 15:20-24, *"²⁰ But now is Christ risen from the dead, and become the firstfruits of them that slept. ²¹For since by man came death, by man came also the resurrection of the dead. ²²For as in Adam all die, even so in Christ shall all be made alive. ²³But every man in his own order: Christ the firstfruits; afterward they that are Christ's at his coming. ²⁴Then cometh the end, when he shall have delivered up the kingdom to God, even the Father; when he shall have put down all rule and all authority and power."*

✝ Matthew 27:52-53, *"⁵²And the graves were opened; and many bodies of the saints which slept arose, ⁵³And came out of the graves after his resurrection, and went into the holy city, and appeared unto many."*

Second: The Rapture is the resurrection of the New Testament Church – meaning those who are in Christ. The dead will rise first before the Tribulation, which was already discussed.

Third: The resurrection of the two witnesses. The scriptures require two or three witnesses to confirm and establish legitimacy of a matter. Two examples are in Deuteronomy 19:15 and Matthew 18:16. During the Tribulation, God will send two prophets known as the two witnesses to confirm sin in the world and prophesy. The two witnesses are spoken of in Revelation 11. The Antichrist will make war with them and kill them. Their bodies will lie in the street for three- and a half days. Their bodies will be seen by the whole world. After which, God will breathe life into them and they will be resurrected and fear will fall on all those who see the two witnesses raptured. The whole world will be watching. This will happen during the Middle of the Tribulation.

✝ Deuteronomy 19:15, *"One witness shall not rise up against a man for any iniquity, or for any sin, in any sin that he sinneth: at the mouth of two witnesses, or at the mouth of three witnesses, shall the matter be established."*

✝ Matthew 18:16, *"But if he will not hear thee, then take with thee one or two more, that in the mouth of two or three witnesses every word may be established."*

✝ Revelation 11:10-13, *"¹⁰And they that dwell upon the earth shall rejoice over them, and make merry, and shall send gifts one to another; because these two prophets tormented them that dwelt on the earth. ¹¹And after three days and an half the spirit of life from God entered into them, and they stood upon their feet; and great fear fell upon them which saw them. ¹²And they heard a great voice from heaven saying unto them, Come up hither. And they ascended up to heaven in a cloud; and their enemies beheld them. ¹³And the same hour was there a great earthquake, and the tenth part of the city fell, and in the earthquake were slain of men seven thousand: and the remnant were affrighted, and gave glory to the God of heaven."*

Fourth: Resurrection of the Old Testament saints. The fourth and fifth resurrection will happen after the Tribulation and prior to the Millennium.

Fifth: Resurrection of the martyrs at the end of the tribulation, which is at the Second Coming.

† Revelation 7:14, *"¹⁴And I said unto him, Sir, thou knowest. And he said to me, These are they which came out of great tribulation, and have washed their robes, and made them white in the blood of the Lamb."*

† Revelation 20:4-5, *"⁴And I saw thrones, and they sat upon them, and judgment was given unto them: and* I saw *the souls of them that were beheaded for the witness of Jesus, and for the word of God, and which had not worshipped the beast, neither his image, neither had received* his *mark upon their foreheads, or in their hands; and they lived and reigned with Christ a thousand years. ⁵ But the rest of the dead lived not again until the thousand years were finished. This* is *the first resurrection."*

The believing survivors of the Tribulation will not be resurrected and will have mortal bodies going into the Millennium. There is much discussion about whether the 144,000 Jews will be resurrected. There is no Scripture that says the 144,000 die. One must die before he/she can be resurrected. Revelation 7:2-3 specifies they are spared from judgment, and they are protected and sealed. The word "sealed" in Revelation 7:3 (Strong's Number 4972) means to stamp, to attest ownership, to authorize or validate. They have been validated and authorized to perform a special work and they cannot be harmed by the Tribulation threats and events.

The 144,000 could have ascended if you interpret Mount Zion as being in heaven. Scripture does not say the 144,000 ascended. Another interpretation of the Mount Zion location is that of a scene-taking place on earth, whether in the New Jerusalem or the earthly Jerusalem during the Millennium. The Mount Zion referred to in Revelation 14:1 is the City of Jerusalem where Jesus will return and plant His feet.

† Matthew 24:13, *"But he that shall endure unto the end, the same shall be saved."*

† Revelation 7:2-3, *"²And I saw another angel ascending from the east, having the seal of the living God: and he cried with a loud voice to the four angels, to whom it was given to hurt the earth and the sea, ³Saying, Hurt not the earth, neither the sea, nor the trees, till we have sealed the servants of our God in their foreheads."*

† Revelation 14:1-5, *"¹And I looked, and, lo, a Lamb stood on the mount Sion, and with him an hundred forty and four thousand, having his Father's name written in their foreheads. ²And I heard a voice from heaven, as the voice of many waters, and as the voice of a great thunder: and I heard the voice of harpers harping with their harps: ³And they sung as it were a new song before the throne, and before the four beasts, and the elders: and no man could learn that song but the hundred and forty and four thousand, which were redeemed from the earth. ⁴These are they which were not defiled with women; for they are virgins. These are they which follow the Lamb whithersoever he goeth. These were redeemed from among men, being the firstfruits unto God and to the Lamb. ⁵And in their mouth was found no guile: for they are without fault before the throne of God."*

Revelation chapters 19-20 do not discuss the Rapture at all. Hence giving the implication that those believers, on earth, which are alive after the Tribulation, at the Second Coming, will go into the Millennium in their mortal bodies.

The 144,000 of Revelation 7 and of Revelation 14 are the same.

The "rest of the dead" refers to those who rejected Jesus as Lord and Savior and as God. They will experience the second resurrection at the end of the Millennium.

† Revelation 6: 9-11, *"⁹And when he had opened the fifth seal, I saw under the altar the souls of them that were slain for the word of God, and for the testimony which they held: ¹⁰ And they cried with a loud*

voice, saying, How long, O Lord, holy and true, do you not judge and avenge our blood on them that dwell on the earth? ¹¹And white robes were given unto every one of them; and it was said unto them, that they should rest yet for a little season, until their fellow servants also and their brethren, that should be killed as they were, should be fulfilled."

The second resurrection is for those who have not repented and who have rejected God. Upon their resurrection they will stand in the final judgment at the end of the Millennium.

† Second Thessalonians 1:9, *"Who shall be punished with everlasting destruction from the presence of the Lord, and from the glory of his power;"*

From the point they died their physical death, those who rejected God can have no other chance to be saved. They will be separated from God forever.

† Revelation 20:12-13, *"¹²And I saw the dead, small and great, stand before God; and the books were opened: and another book was opened, which is the book of life: and the dead were judged out of those things which were written in the books, according to their works. ¹³And the sea gave up the dead which were in it; and death and hell delivered up the dead which were in them: and they were judged every man according to their works."*

MAJOR RESURRECTIONS

<table>
<tr><td colspan="5" align="center">FIRST RESURRECTION
FOR THE SAVED (JUST)</td></tr>
<tr>
<td>1.

Past- After the death of Jesus</td>
<td>2.

At the Rapture</td>
<td>3.

Middle of the Tribulation</td>
<td>4.

At the end of Tribulation Prior to Millennium</td>
<td>5.

At the end of Tribulation Prior to Millennium</td>
</tr>
<tr>
<td>Jesus and some Old Testament Jerusalem saints</td>
<td>Resurrection of the Church Dead rise first Then those alive in Christ</td>
<td>Resurrection of the two witnesses</td>
<td>Resurrection of the Old Testament saints</td>
<td>Resurrection of the martyrs (Tribulation Saints) at the end of the Tribulation, which is at the Second Coming</td>
</tr>
<tr>
<td>Matthew 27:52-53 Matthew 28:1-7; Mark 16:1-11; Luke 24:1-12; John 20:1-18; First Corinthians 15:20-24</td>
<td>John 14:3; First Thessalonians 4:17-18; First Corinthians 15:50-53; Second Corinthians 5:1-4</td>
<td>Revelation 11:10-13</td>
<td>Ezekiel 37: 12-14; Daniel 12:1-2; Revelation 20:4</td>
<td>Daniel 12:1-2; Revelation 20:4-5; Revelation 6:9-11</td>
</tr>
</table>

**The believing survivors of the Tribulation and the 144,000 Jews will not be resurrected and will have mortal bodies going into the Millennium. Matthew 24:13, "[13] But he that shall endure unto the end, the same shall be saved." Revelation chapters 19-20 do not discuss the Rapture at all. This gives the implication that those believers, on earth, which are alive, at the Second Coming, will go into the Millennium in their mortal bodies.

<table>
<tr><td align="center">SECOND RESURRECTION
RESURRECTION OF DAMNATION
RESURRECTION OF THE WICKED

FOR THE UNSAVED (UNJUST)</td></tr>
</table>

<table>
<tr><td>Unsaved – Their souls go to hell after death but their bodies will be raised at end of 1000 year reign of Christ – the end of the Millennium. Their bodies have been partners in sin with their soul and will be judged at the Great White Throne Judgment.

 Daniel 12:1-2
John 5:28-29
Acts 24: 14-15
Second Thessalonians 1:9
Revelation 20:4, 12-15 </td></tr>
</table>

REFERENCED SCRIPTURES

✝ Ezekiel 37: 12-14, *"¹²Therefore prophesy and say unto them, Thus saith the Lord GOD; Behold, O my people, I will open your graves, and cause you to come up out of your graves, and bring you into the land of Israel. ¹³And ye shall know that I am the LORD, when I have opened your graves, O my people, and brought you up out of your graves, ¹⁴And shall put my spirit in you, and ye shall live, and I shall place you in your own land: then shall ye know that I the LORD have spoken it, and performed it, saith the LORD."*

✝ Daniel 12:1-2, *"¹And at that time shall Michael stand up, the great prince which standeth for the children of thy people: and there shall be a time of trouble, such as never was since there was a nation even to that same time: and at that time thy people shall be delivered, every one that shall be found written in the book. ²And many of them that sleep in the dust of the earth shall awake, some to everlasting life, and some to shame and everlasting contempt."*

✝ Matthew 27:52-53, *"⁵²And the graves were opened; and many bodies of the saints which slept arose, ⁵³And came out of the graves after his resurrection, and went into the holy city, and appeared unto many."*

✝ Matthew 28:1-7, *"¹In the end of the sabbath, as it began to dawn toward the first day of the week, came Mary Magdalene and the other Mary to see the sepulchre. ²And, behold, there was a great earthquake: for the angel of the Lord descended from heaven, and came and rolled back the stone from the door, and sat upon it. ³His countenance was like lightning, and his raiment white as snow: ⁴And for fear of him the keepers did shake, and became as dead men. ⁵And the angel answered and said unto the women, Fear not ye: for I know that ye seek Jesus, which was crucified. ⁶He is not here: for he is risen, as he said. Come, see the place where the Lord lay. ⁷And go quickly, and tell his disciples that he is risen from the dead; and, behold, he goeth before you into Galilee; there shall ye see him: lo, I have told you."*

✝ Mark 16:1-11, *"¹And when the sabbath was past, Mary Magdalene, and Mary the mother of James, and Salome, had bought sweet spices, that they might come and anoint him. ²And very early in the morning* the first day of the week, they came unto the sepulchre at the rising of the sun. ³And they said among themselves, Who shall roll us away the stone from the door of the sepulchre? ⁴And when they looked, they saw that the stone was rolled away: for it was very great. ⁵And entering into the sepulchre, they saw a young man sitting on the right side, clothed in a long white garment; and they were affrighted. ⁶And he saith unto them, Be not affrighted: Ye seek Jesus of Nazareth, which was crucified: he is risen; he is not here: behold the place where they laid him. ⁷But go your way, tell his disciples and Peter that he goeth before you into Galilee: there shall ye see him, as he said unto you. ⁸And they went out quickly, and fled from the sepulchre; for they trembled and were amazed: neither said they any thing to any man; for they were afraid. ⁹Now when Jesus was risen early the first day of the week, he appeared first to Mary Magdalene, out of whom he had cast seven devils. ¹⁰And she went and told them that had been with him, as they mourned and wept. ¹¹And they, when they had heard that he was alive, and had been seen of her, believed not"

✝ Luke 24:1-12, "¹Now upon the first day of the week, very early in the morning, they came unto the sepulchre, bringing the spices which they had prepared, and certain others with them. ²And they found the stone rolled away from the sepulchre. ³And they entered in, and found not the body of the Lord Jesus. ⁴And it came to pass, as they were much perplexed thereabout, behold, two men stood by them in shining garments: ⁵And as they were afraid, and bowed down their faces to the earth, they said unto them, Why seek ye the living among the dead? ⁶He is not here, but is risen: remember how he spake unto you when he was yet in Galilee, ⁷Saying, The Son of man must be delivered into the hands of sinful men, and be crucified, and the third day rise again. ⁸And they remembered his words, ⁹And returned from the sepulchre, and told all these things unto the eleven, and to all the rest. ¹⁰It was Mary Magdalene and Joanna, and Mary the mother of James, and other women that were with them, which told these things unto the apostles. ¹¹And their words seemed to them as idle tales, and they believed them not. ¹²Then arose Peter, and ran unto the sepulchre; and stooping down, he beheld the linen clothes laid *by themselves, and departed, wondering in himself at that which was come to pass."*

✝ John 5:28-29, *"[28]Marvel not at this: for the hour is coming, in the which all that are in the graves shall hear his voice, [29]And shall come forth; they that have done good, unto the resurrection of life; and they that have done evil, unto the resurrection of damnation."*

✝ John 14:3, *"And if I go and prepare a place for you, I will come again, and receive you unto myself; that where I am, there ye may be also."*

✝ John 20:1-18, *"[1]The first day of the week cometh Mary Magdalene early, when it was yet dark, unto the sepulchre, and seeth the stone taken away from the sepulchre. [2]Then she runneth, and cometh to Simon Peter, and to the other disciple, whom Jesus loved, and saith unto them, They have taken away the Lord out of the sepulchre, and we know not where they have laid him. [3]Peter therefore went forth, and that other disciple, and came to the sepulchre. [4]So they ran both together: and the other disciple did outrun Peter, and came first to the sepulchre. [5]And he stooping down, and looking in, saw the linen clothes lying; yet went he not in. [6]Then cometh Simon Peter following him, and went into the sepulchre, and seeth the linen clothes lie, [7]And the napkin, that was about his head, not lying with the linen clothes, but wrapped together in a place by itself. [8]Then went in also that other disciple, which came first to the sepulchre, and he saw, and believed. [9]For as yet they knew not the scripture, that he must rise again from the dead. [10]Then the disciples went away again unto their own home. [11]But Mary stood without at the sepulchre weeping: and as she wept, she stooped down, and looked into the sepulchre, [12]And seeth two angels in white sitting, the one at the head, and the other at the feet, where the body of Jesus had lain. [13]And they say unto her, Woman, why weepest thou? She saith unto them, Because they have taken away my Lord, and I know not where they have laid him. [14]And when she had thus said, she turned herself back, and saw Jesus standing, and knew not that it was Jesus. [15]Jesus saith unto her, Woman, why weepest thou? whom seekest thou? She, supposing him to be the gardener, saith unto him, Sir, if thou have borne him hence, tell me where thou hast laid him, and I will take him away. [16]Jesus saith unto* her, Mary. She turned herself, and saith unto him, Rabboni; which is to say, Master. *17Jesus saith unto her, Touch me not; for I am not yet ascended to my Father: but go to my brethren, and say unto them, I ascend unto my Father, and your Father; and to my God, and your God. 18Mary Magdalene came and told the disciples that she had seen the LORD, and that he had spoken these things unto her.*

† Acts 24:14-15, *"14But this I confess unto thee, that after the way which they call heresy, so worship I the God of my fathers, believing all things which are written in the law and in the prophets: 15And have hope toward God, which they themselves also allow, that there shall be a resurrection of the dead, both of the just and unjust."*

† First Corinthians 15:20-24, *"20But now is Christ risen from the dead, and become the firstfruits of them that slept. 21For since by man came death, by man came also the resurrection of the dead. 22For as in Adam all die, even so in Christ shall all be made alive. 23But every man in his own order: Christ the firstfruits; afterward they that are Christ's at his coming. 24Then cometh the end, when he shall have delivered up the kingdom to God, even the Father; when he shall have put down all rule and all authority and power."*

† First Corinthians 15:50-53, *"50Now this I say, brethren, that flesh and blood cannot inherit the kingdom of God; neither doth corruption inherit incorruption. 51Behold, I shew you a mystery; We shall not all sleep, but we shall all be changed, 52In a moment, in the twinkling of an eye, at the last trump: for the trumpet shall sound, and the dead shall be raised incorruptible, and we shall be changed. 53For this corruptible must put on incorruption, and this mortal must put on immortality."*

† Second Corinthians 5:1-4, *"1For we know that if our earthly house of this tabernacle were dissolved, we have a building of God, an house not made with hands, eternal in the heavens. 2For in this we groan, earnestly desiring to be clothed upon with our house which is from heaven: 3If so be that being clothed we shall not be found naked. 4For we that are in this tabernacle do groan, being burdened: not for that we would be unclothed, but clothed upon, that mortality might be swallowed up of life."*

✝ First Thessalonians 4:17-18, *"¹⁷Then we which are alive and remain shall be caught up together with them in the clouds, to meet the Lord in the air: and so shall we ever be with the Lord." ¹⁸Wherefore comfort one another with these words."*

✝ Second Thessalonians 1:9, *"Who shall be punished with everlasting destruction from the presence of the Lord, and from the glory of his power;"*

✝ Revelation 6:9-11, *"⁹And when he had opened the fifth seal, I saw under the altar the souls of them that were slain for the word of God, and for the testimony which they held: ¹⁰And they cried with a loud voice, saying, How long, O Lord, holy and true, dost thou not judge and avenge our blood on them that dwell on the earth? ¹¹And white robes were given unto every one of them; and it was said unto them, that they should rest yet for a little season, until their fellowservants also and their brethren, that should be killed as they were, should be fulfilled."*

✝ Revelation 11:10-13, *"¹⁰And they that dwell upon the earth shall rejoice over them, and make merry, and shall send gifts one to another; because these two prophets tormented them that dwelt on the earth. ¹¹And after three days and an half the spirit of life from God entered into them, and they stood upon their feet; and great fear fell upon them which saw them. ¹²And they heard a great voice from heaven saying unto them, Come up hither. And they ascended up to heaven in a cloud; and their enemies beheld them. ¹³And the same hour was there a great earthquake, and the tenth part of the city fell, and in the earthquake were slain of men seven thousand: and the remnant were affrighted, and gave glory to the God of heaven."*

✝ Revelation 20: 4-5, *"And I saw thrones, and they sat upon them, and judgment was given unto them: and I saw the souls of them that were beheaded for the witness of Jesus, and for the word of God, and which had not worshipped the beast, neither his image, neither had received his mark upon their foreheads, or in their hands; and they lived and reigned with Christ a thousand years. ⁵But the rest of the dead lived not again until the thousand years were finished. This is the first resurrection."*

† Revelation 20: 12-15, "*[12] And I saw the dead, small and great, stand before God; and the books were opened: and another book was opened, which is the book of life: and the dead were judged out of those things which were written in the books, according to their works. [13] And the sea gave up the dead which were in it; and death and hell delivered up the dead which were in them: and they were judged every man according to their works. [14] And death and hell were cast into the lake of fire. This is the second death. [15] And whosoever was not found written in the book of life was cast into the lake of fire.*"

PERSONAL NOTES

CHAPTER EIGHT

REWARDS AND PUNISHMENTS

God promises to reward everyone according to his/her works (Revelation 22:12). The word rewards refers in the sense of both rewards and punishments. Rewards will be allocated according to what we have sown whether good or bad.

Everyone, even believers, have to give an account to God.

† Romans 14:10-12, *"¹⁰But why dost thou judge thy brother? or why dost thou set at nought thy brother? for we shall all stand before the Judgment Seat of Christ. ¹¹For it is written, As I live, saith the Lord, every knee shall bow to me, and every tongue shall confess to God. ¹²So then every one of us shall give account of himself to God."*

† Second Corinthians 5:10, *"For we must all appear before the Judgment Seat of Christ; that every one may receive the things done in his body, according to that he hath done, whether it be good or bad."*

† Revelation 22:12, *"And, behold, I come quickly; and my reward is with me, to give every man according as his work shall be."*

There are two end time judgments. One is the Judgment Seat of Christ and the other is the Great White Throne Judgment. One is the believer's judgment, which will be different than the non-believers' judgment. They occur at different times and for two different groups. Those who accept Jesus as their Lord and Savior will appear before the Judgment Seat of Christ. The believer will be judged according to his/her works. This judgment occurs after the Rapture in heaven. The Judgment Seat is also called the Bema seat judgment. Bema (# 968 Strong's Concordance) is the Greek word for Judgment Seat and means *step*. It implies an elevated stage for the Judge during the judicial proceedings or the official seat of the judge. Those who don't accept Jesus, as Lord, will be judged at the Great White Throne Judgment. The Great White Throne Judgment occurs after the Millennium for the unrepentant sinner. Those will be given the death sentence (eternal separation from God) in the Lake of Fire.

✝ First Corinthians 3:12-15, *"¹²Now if any man build upon this foundation gold, silver, precious stones, wood, hay, stubble; ¹³Every man's work shall be made manifest: for the day shall declare it, because it shall be revealed by fire; and the fire shall try every man's work of what sort it is. ¹⁴If any man's work abide which he hath built thereupon, he shall receive a reward. ¹⁵If any man's work shall be burned, he shall suffer loss: but he himself shall be saved; yet so as by fire."*

Only the redeemed of the Lord will stand before the Judgment Seat of Christ. After the Rapture, the believer will be "judged". This judgment has nothing to do with our salvation. Salvation comes only by grace and through faith and not by works (Ephesians 2: 8-9). Only through the atoning work of Christ Jesus can salvation be obtained.

The Judgment Seat for the believer is not for the purpose of condemnation.

✝ Romans 8:1, *"There is therefore now no condemnation to them which are in Christ Jesus, who walk not after the flesh, but after the Spirit."*

JOY KARANICK ROACH

This judgment will be to reward believers for their works, for what they have done for Christ. Believers will be rewarded based on how faithfully they served Jesus and others.

- † There are varying degrees of rewards as taught by Jesus in the parable of talents in Luke 19:12-27.
- † First Corinthians 3:8, *"Now he that planteth and he that watereth are one: and every man shall receive his own reward according to his own labour."*

Jesus promised various rewards for those who will faithfully serve Him.

- † Matthew 5:12, *"Rejoice, and be exceeding glad: for great is your reward in heaven: for so persecuted they the prophets which were before you."*
- † First Corinthians 3:14, *"If any man's work abide which he hath built thereupon, he shall receive a reward."*
- † Revelation 22:12, *"And, behold, I come quickly; and my reward is with me, to give every man according as his work shall be."*

Some of those rewards will be crowns, which we will cast at the feet of Jesus. The Greek word for crown is *stephanoo* (Strong's # 4737) and implies the winner or victor in a contest. It was used as a symbol of victory over death taken from the Roman Goddess Victoria. Victory is Latin for Victoria. A crown was also used as a symbol of victory in Greek games and contests.

- † Revelation 4:10-11, *"¹⁰The four and twenty elders fall down before him that sat on the throne, and worship him that liveth for ever and ever, and cast their crowns before the throne, saying, ¹¹Thou art worthy, O Lord, to receive glory and honour and power: for thou hast created all things, and for thy pleasure they are and were created."*

Crowns will be one of the types of rewards given to believers. Crowns are a symbol of eternal rewards for victory, righteousness, kingship, triumph, honor, and glory. The Bible speaks of five crowns that believers will receive in heaven.

1. An Incorruptible or Imperishable Crown also called Victor's crown for self-discipline and mastery over the sin nature of humanity.

> † First Corinthians 9:25-27, *"²⁵And every man that striveth for the mastery is temperate in all things. Now they do it to obtain a corruptible crown; but we an incorruptible. ²⁶I therefore so run, not as uncertainly; so fight I, not as one that beateth the air: ²⁷But I keep under my body, and bring it into subjection: lest that by any means, when I have preached to others, I myself should be a castaway."*
> † Second Timothy 2:5, *"And if a man also strive for masteries, yet is he not crowned, except he strive lawfully."*

2. A Crown of Rejoicing also known as a soul winner's crown.

> † First Thessalonians 2:10, *"Ye are witnesses, and God also, how holily and justly and unblameably we behaved ourselves among you that believe:" "¹⁹. For what is our hope, or joy, or crown of rejoicing? Are not even ye in the presence of our Lord Jesus Christ at his coming?"*

3. A Crown of Righteousness for all those who long for Him, keep the faith, and look forward to His return.

> † Second Timothy 4:7-8, *"⁷I have fought a good fight, I have finished my course, I have kept the faith: ⁸Henceforth there is laid up for me a crown of righteousness, which the Lord, the righteous judge, shall give me at that day: and not to me only, but unto all them also that love his appearing."*

4. A Crown of Life for those who endured temptation and trials.

> † James 1:12, *"Blessed is the man that endureth temptation: for when he is tried, he shall receive the crown of life, which the Lord hath promised to them that love him."*

† Revelation 2:10, *"Fear none of those things which thou shalt suffer: behold, the devil shall cast some of you into prison, that ye may be tried; and ye shall have tribulation ten days: be thou faithful unto death, and I will give thee a crown of life."*

5. A Crown of Glory for faithful shepherds.

† First Peter 5:4, *"And when the chief Shepherd shall appear, ye shall receive a crown of glory that fadeth not away.*

The sinner's destiny and reward is to be cast into the Lake of Fire----Hell. Believers are to teach, preach, witness, and live the life of holiness so that the Truth of His Word might convict them. If sinners might repent before it is too late, they can be saved from the Tribulation and the Lake of Fire. Revelation 20: 7-15 details the time of the Great White Throne Judgment and the events.

† Revelation 20:7-15, *"⁷And when the thousand years are expired, Satan shall be loosed out of his prison, ⁸And shall go out to deceive the nations which are in the four quarters of the earth, Gog, and Magog, to gather them together to battle: the number of whom is as the sand of the sea. ⁹And they went up on the breadth of the earth, and compassed the camp of the saints about, and the beloved city: and fire came down from God out of heaven, and devoured them. ¹⁰And the devil that deceived them was cast into the lake of fire and brimstone, where the beast and the false prophet are, and shall be tormented day and night for ever and ever. ¹¹And I saw a great white throne, and him that sat on it, from whose face the earth and the heaven fled away; and there was found no place for them. ¹²And I saw the dead, small and great, stand before God; and the books were opened: and another book was opened, which is the book of life: and the dead were judged out of those things which were written in the books, according to their works. ¹³And the sea gave up the dead which were in it; and death and hell delivered up the dead which were in them: and they were judged every man according to their works. ¹⁴And death and hell were cast*

into the lake of fire. This is the second death. ¹⁵And whosoever was not found written in the book of life was cast into the lake of fire."

RECOMMENDED ACTIVITIES

1. Look up "Judgment Seat" in Greek in the Strong's Concordance. How many times is it used? What is the Greek word for it? How is it used in the ten scriptures? How does it differ and how does it relate to the place of judgment for believers in the end times?
2. Study the bema seat where judges awarded athletes for their performance in the city of Corinth.
3. Study the five crowns and find other scriptures that may speak about them. Try looking up the word *crown* in Strong's Concordance and that will be a great start. How many times is the word found in the Bible? Does each word have the same meaning? Compare any references to the crown in the Old Testament especially how it was used with Kings.

PERSONAL NOTES

CHAPTER NINE

THE TRIBULATION

Matthew 24:15-21

"¹⁵When ye therefore shall see the abomination of desolation, spoken of by Daniel the prophet, stand in the holy place, (whoso readeth, let him understand:) ¹⁶Then let them which be in Judaea flee into the mountains: ¹⁷Let him which is on the housetop not come down to take any thing out of his house: ¹⁸Neither let him which is in the field return back to take his clothes. ¹⁹And woe unto them that are with child, and to them that give suck in those days! ²⁰But pray ye that your flight be not in the winter, neither on the sabbath day: ²¹For then shall be great tribulation, such as was not since the beginning of the world to this time, no, nor ever shall be."

The Tribulation on earth will begin after the Church is raptured. The Tribulation will be a time on earth when God will pour out His wrath for those who rejected Him. John wrote:

✝ Revelation 6:17, *"For the great day of his wrath is come; and who shall be able to stand?"*

The abomination of desolation spoken of by Daniel and referred to by Matthew and Luke is a warning! A warning that is relevant for

90

us today. The phrase can also refer to the image of the Antichrist in the Temple. Some say Matthew refers to when Antiochus Epiphanes desecrated the Temple during the intertestamental period of 400 years of silence and about 200 years before Christ. The phrase *abomination of desolation* means a foul or detestable thing or hateful things that destroy, makes desolate or lays waste, and strips of treasures. In its context in Matthew, this phrase not only refers to the destruction of the temple in 70 AD by the Romans but also warned to avoid the disturbing persecution and horrific events of the Tribulation.

The effect of the Rapture will initially trigger utter and complete chaos on earth. Imagine it for yourself. Two people who drove the train, both were saved believers in Jesus Christ and suddenly they are caught up in the air. The train has no driver. The same goes for an airplane. There were two pilots and only one of them was saved. Bam! The saved pilot goes missing and the unsaved pilot was left behind. How about at the air traffic control towers? How about at the communication centers, the financial systems, the hospitals, cars, and buses? Wrecks, overloaded telephone systems or lack of a telephone system over the world. Many graves will open, fires and looting breakout everywhere. Every system in the world instantly fails. People will look for answers. Cults, false prophets, and churches will arise but no one will be able to offer peace. At this time the Antichrist will arise but will not reveal himself as the Antichrist. No one will realize he is the Antichrist until he reveals himself at the middle of the Tribulation. He will speak peace and attempt to calm everyone over the world. People will flock to him and his pseudo peace. He will set up the one-world government and sign a peace treaty with Israel.

The Tribulation period will last seven years. Part one will last for three-and one-half years and part two, called the Great Tribulation, will be the worst time for three- and one-half more years. Part two known as the Great Tribulation is also called the Middle of the Week. The Bible refers to the Tribulation by other names as well.

"Day of the Lord" is frequently used in the Old and New Testaments to refer to the Tribulation period. These are just a few of the many passages found in Scripture.

† Isaiah 2:12, *"For the day of the LORD of hosts shall be upon every one that is proud and lofty, and upon every one that is lifted up; and he shall be brought low:"*

† Joel 1:15, *"Alas for the day! for the day of the LORD is at hand, and as a destruction from the Almighty shall it come."*

† Malachi 4:5, *"Behold, I will send you Elijah the prophet before the coming of the great and dreadful day of the LORD:"*

† Acts 2:20, *"The sun shall be turned into darkness, and the moon into blood, before that great and notable day of the Lord come:"*

† First Corinthians 5:5, *"To deliver such an one unto Satan for the destruction of the flesh, that the spirit may be saved in the day of the Lord Jesus."*

The "Time of the End" in Daniel refers to the "End of Times" for Gentiles but not the final end of the world. It is the time when the Antichrist will rule and take authority when the "Times of the Gentiles" are fulfilled. The city of Babylon began the "Times of the Gentiles" in which the Antichrist is called the King of Babylon in Isaiah 14:4. The "Time of the Gentiles" in Luke 21:24 refers politically to the time Israel is under the domination of Gentile rule. It began at the Babylonian Captivity and will end at the Second Coming. The "Fullness of the Gentiles" in Romans 11:25 is different. It has more to do with numbers not politics. Fullness of the Gentiles is referring to when the last person becomes part of the Church before she is raptured. It began on the day of Pentecost when the Church was born and will end at the Rapture. That is seven years before the Time of the Gentiles ends at the Second Coming.

† Daniel 12:9, *"And he said, Go thy way, Daniel: for the words are closed up and sealed till the time of the end."*

† Isaiah 14:4, *"That thou shalt take up this proverb against the king of Babylon, and say, How hath the oppressor ceased! the golden city ceased!*

† Luke 21:24, *"And they shall fall by the edge of the sword, and shall be led away captive into all nations: and Jerusalem shall be trodden down of the Gentiles, until the times of the Gentiles be fulfilled."*

† Romans 11:25, *"For I would not, brethren, that ye should be ignorant of this mystery, lest ye should be wise in your own conceits; that blindness in part is happened to Israel, until the fulness of the Gentiles be come in."*

The phrase, "End of the World" can refer to the Tribulation period.

† Matthew 13:40, *"As therefore the tares are gathered and burned in the fire; so shall it be in the end of this world."*

† Matthew 13:49, *"So shall it be at the end of the world: the angels shall come forth, and sever the wicked from among the just,"*

The phrase, "The Time of Jacob's Trouble" refers to the Tribulation.

† Jeremiah 30:7, *"Alas! for that day is great, so that none is like it: it is even the time of Jacob's trouble, but he shall be saved out of it."*

The "Day of the Lord's Wrath" and "Day of Trouble and Distress" refers to the Tribulation in the book of Zephaniah.

† Zephaniah 1:15, *"That day is a day of wrath, a day of trouble and distress, a day of wasteness and desolation, a day of darkness and gloominess, a day of clouds and thick darkness,*

† Zephaniah 1:18, *"Neither their silver nor their gold shall be able to deliver them in the day of the Lord's wrath; but the whole land shall be devoured by the fire of his jealousy: for he shall make even a speedy riddance of all them that dwell in the land."*

The Tribulation is also called, "The Hour of Trial" and the "Hour of His Judgment" in Revelation.

† Revelation 3:10, *"Because thou hast kept the word of my patience, I also will keep thee from the hour of temptation, which shall come upon all the world, to try them that dwell upon the earth."*

† Revelation 14:7, *"Saying with a loud voice, Fear God, and give glory to him; for the hour of his judgment is come: and worship him that made heaven, and earth, and the sea, and the fountains of waters."*

"Indignation" refers to the Tribulation.

† Isaiah 26:20, *"Come, my people, enter thou into thy chambers, and shut thy doors about thee: hide thyself as it were for a little moment, until the indignation be overpast."*

The seven-year Tribulation period is referred to as "seventy weeks".

† Daniel 9:24-27, *"[24]Seventy weeks are determined upon thy people and upon thy holy city, to finish the transgression, and to make an end of sins, and to make reconciliation for iniquity, and to bring in everlasting righteousness, and to seal up the vision and prophecy, and to anoint the most Holy. [25]Know therefore and understand, that from the going forth of the commandment to restore and to build Jerusalem unto the Messiah the Prince shall be seven weeks, and threescore and two weeks: the street shall be built again, and the wall, even in troublous times. [26]And after threescore and two weeks shall Messiah be cut off, but not for himself: and the people of the prince that shall come shall destroy the city and the sanctuary; and the end thereof shall be with a flood, and unto the end of the war desolations are determined. [27]And he shall confirm the covenant with many for one week: and in the midst of the week he shall cause the sacrifice and the oblation to cease, and for the overspreading of abominations he shall make it desolate, even until the consummation, and that determined shall be poured upon the desolate."*

Daniel's Messianic prophecy (Daniel 9: 24-27) summarizes some of the events before the Millennium. His prophecy is the basis for how "Pre-Tribulationists" determine the Tribulation lasts for seven years. Some of the prophecy is fulfilled and some is yet to come. The Tribulation or the Seventieth Week cannot happen until a seven-year treaty is signed between Israel and the Antichrist and the temple is rebuilt. Second Thessalonians 2:4 tells us that the Antichrist will sit in the temple and proclaim to be God. Matthew 24:15 refers to the holy place which is part of the temple. Currently there is no temple. This must be fulfilled before the seventy weeks can transpire.

- † Matthew 24:15, *"When ye therefore shall see the abomination of desolation, spoken of by Daniel the prophet, stand in the holy place, (whoso readeth, let him understand:)"*
- † Second Thessalonians 2:4, *"Who opposeth and exalteth himself above all that is called God, or that is worshipped; so that he as God sitteth in the temple of God, shewing himself that he is God."*

The prophecy revealed that Jesus had to be crucified and the temple had to be destroyed. These two events happened. The temple was destroyed in 70 AD. Israel had to become united as a nation. Israel, then know as Palestine, was under the British rule between 1917 and 1948. In May, 1948 Israel became the Jewish nation. The temple still has to be rebuilt. Sacrifices and offerings have to be reinstated. This part of the prophecy has not been fulfilled yet. The Antichrist will promise to protect Israel in the treaty. However, He will defy the treaty during the middle of the Tribulation and will end all animal sacrifices and offerings (Daniel 9:27).

A short discussion about the tabernacle/ and temple is important to insert here. The first place of worship in the Bible was the Tabernacle of Moses. God wanted to be in the midst of His people. Exodus 25-40 describes the Tabernacle and its furniture. Each piece of furniture points us to Christ. The place of the Tabernacle had three sections: the outer court, the Holy Place or the Inner Court and the Most Holy Place or the Holy of Holies. The outer court had two pieces of furniture. One was the brazen altar or the altar of sacrifice. Animal sacrifices were placed on the altar and the blood would be collected for the Priest to sprinkle in the Most Holy Place for the remission of the sins of the people. Jesus Christ was our ultimate sacrifice and today no other sacrifice is needed nor could even measure up to the sacrifice He made for us. Another furniture piece in the outer court was the brazen laver. This was a water basin for the Priests to wash before they enter into the Holy Place. Mirrors lined the basin, which reflected the image of the Priests. It symbolizes washing before entering. We want to stand clean before the Lord Jesus and after we have received the sacrifice of our Lord, we reflect through the mirrors on our past, our sins, and our life. Then and only then we can enter into the Holy Place. Only Priests were allowed into this section. There were three pieces of furniture inside. One was a table of showbread, whereby one loaf from each tribe was place. Every Sabbath the bread would be replaced. The Priests would eat from this bread during the week. The bread represents Jesus because the scriptures say He is the bread of life. Secondly, there was a menorah or a lampstand. This provided light for the sanctuary. Jesus is the light of the world and has commanded us to put on the armor of light and to be a light in this world. Thirdly, the altar of incense represented the prayers of the saints.

The Holy of Holies is the third section, which could be entered only by the High Priest and only once a year on Yom Kippur (day of atonement). A solid curtain without openings separated the Holy Place and the Most Holy Place. The High Priest would there atone for the sins of the people and reconcile them back to God. The Ark of the Covenant was its only piece of furniture. The Ark represents the presence of God. This is the place God would speak to His people. On top of the Ark was the mercy seat where God would appear as a cloud by day and a pillar of fire by night to guide the Israelites during their Egyptian bondage. It represented God's involvement with His people. When Christ died for us and became the final sacrifice for the atoning of sins, the solid curtain tore. This represents that we all now have access to His presence. We can all enter into the Holy of Holies. We have no go between for the atoning of our sins. We all can go to Him in prayer and ask forgiveness because of His blood.

The moveable tent of meeting, the tabernacle, was eventually put to rest. The Temple became the worship place and housed the same kind of furnishings as the Tabernacle.

A Temple did not exist until the time when Israel called out for a King instead of judges. God was unhappy about this demand but nonetheless appointed Saul as the first King over Israel. After King Saul, King David was anointed by God to be the King of Israel. David wanted to build a house for God. He was told that he could not do so because he had blood on his hands. God assured David that his son Solomon would build the Temple. The first Temple built in 957 BC was called Solomon's Temple. It was extravagant and extremely luxurious. Solomon's Temple was destroyed in 586 B.C. when King Nebuchadnezzar conquered Jerusalem as Jeremiah had prophesied. King Nebuchadnezzar held the Jews in captivity for seventy years in Babylon. Babylonian captivity ended when King Cyrus from Persia attacked Babylon and released the Jews allowing them to return home and worship their God. Isaiah prophcsicd this about one hundred years before King Cyrus. The Jews left in three groups at three different times while some remained in Persia. The book of Nehemiah describes one return and the rebuilding of the wall around Jerusalem. The book of Ezra describes the rebuilding of the Temple under Zerubbabel. Esther was one of the ones who remained in Persia and she became the Queen to King Ahasuerus. Later under King Herod, the King during the birth of Christ renovated the Temple to make it more elaborate. That Temple was called King Herod's Temple or the Second Temple. It was in this Temple that Jesus taught. King Herod's Temple was destroyed in 70 AD. Jesus foretold the destruction of this Temple in the book of Mark. The only portion left of the Temple is the Wailing Wall where Jews and tourists go to pray. Currently there is no Temple so sacrifices cannot be made and the High Priest cannot enter into the Holy of Holies to atone for the sins of the people. The Dome of the Rock, a Muslim mosque, sits on top of the Temple Mount. This poses some dialogue about how the building of the Tribulation Temple can take place without a war. The Antichrist will sit on the throne in the Tribulation Temple. In the new heaven and new earth, there will be no need for a physical Temple (Revelation 21).

The Tabernacle and Temple was a place to meet with God, a place where He dwelled. The Ark of the Covenant and the glory cloud represented his presence. In the new heaven and new earth, God's presence will be everywhere.

Now we can continue with the explanation of Daniel's seventy weeks. A few calculation conversions are necessary to understand Daniel's prophetic word regarding seventy weeks. Refer to the chart below for calculation definitions. It is necessary to see the definitions of seventy weeks before realizing how Daniel's prophecy is broken out and calculated.

SEVENTY WEEKS
Daniel 9:24-27

DURATION	EQUALS	CALCULATION	SCRIPTURE
One day	=	One year	Numbers 14:34 Ezekiel 4:6
One week	=	Seven years	
Seventy weeks	=	Four hundred and ninety years	Daniel 9:24-27
One score	=	Twenty	
Three score and two weeks	=	Sixty-two weeks	Daniel 9:25-26
Sixty-two weeks	=	Four hundred and thirty four years	Daniel 9: 26
One thousand two hundred and sixty days	=	Forty-two months	Daniel 7:25 Revelation 11:2-3 Revelation 12:6 Revelation 13:5
A Time	=	One year	
Half Time	=	One-half year	
Time, times, and a half time (Or dividing of times)	=	Three and one-half years	Daniel 7:25 Daniel 12:7 Revelation 12:14
Middle (midst) of the week	=	Three and one-half years	Daniel 9:27
Forty-two months	=	Three and one-half years	Revelation 11:2 Revelation 13:5
Time, times, and a half time	=	Twelve hundred and sixty days	Revelation 11:3 Revelation 12:6
One month	=	Thirty days (As used by Jews)	
One year	=	Three hundred and sixty days (as used by Jews)	

Daniel's prophecy of seventy weeks breaks out into three phases in Scripture. The first two phases have been fulfilled. The third phase is still future.

1. First Phase = Time of restoration and repair of Jerusalem post Babylonian exile:

Seven weeks = forty-nine years (One week equals seven years)

2. Second Phase = Time from Zerubbabel rebuilding the Temple in the Book of Ezra to the crucifixion of Christ:

Sixty-two weeks = four hundred and thirty four years (Daniel 9:26)

First phase + Second Phase = 49 years + 434 years = 483 years (have been fulfilled)

3. Third Phase = Tribulation:

70 weeks or 490 years – 483 years = 1 week or 7 years of Tribulation (still to be fulfilled)

What exactly will happen during these seven years of Tribulation? Daniel did not understand completely but what he knew was a time of trouble was coming. He was told then to seal up the books but now the mystery has been revealed through Apostle John. It is no longer a mystery! The Book of Revelation details the events of the Tribulation. There will be judgments poured out upon the earth. These judgments occur in three groups and each group contains seven. The judgments are called seals, trumpets, and vials (or bowls). Each judgment grows progressively worse. The middle of the week or at three and a half years of judgment during the Tribulation the Antichrist will reveal himself. Then the judgments become even more painful as the wrath increasingly intensifies. The middle of the week or at three and a half years is called the Great Tribulation.

REFERENCED SCRIPTURES

† Numbers 14:34, *"After the number of the days in which ye searched the land, even forty days, each day for a year, shall ye bear your iniquities, even forty years, and ye shall know my breach of promise."*

† Ezekiel 4:6, *"And when thou hast accomplished them, lie again on thy right side, and thou shalt bear the iniquity of the house of Judah forty days: I have appointed thee each day for a year."*

† Daniel 7:25, *"And he shall speak great words against the most High, and shall wear out the saints of the most High, and think to change times and laws: and they shall be given into his hand until a time and times and the dividing of time."*

† Daniel 9:24-27, *"²⁴Seventy weeks are determined upon thy people and upon thy holy city, to finish the transgression, and to make an end of sins, and to make reconciliation for iniquity, and to bring in everlasting righteousness, and to seal up the vision and prophecy, and to anoint the most Holy. ²⁵Know therefore and understand, that from the going forth of the commandment to restore and to build Jerusalem unto the Messiah the Prince shall be seven weeks, and threescore and two weeks: the street shall be built again, and the wall, even in troublous times. ²⁶And after threescore and two weeks shall Messiah be cut off, but not for himself: and the people of the prince that shall come shall destroy the city and the sanctuary; and the end thereof shall be with a flood, and unto the end of the war desolations are determined. ²⁷And he shall confirm the covenant with many for one week: and in the midst of the week he shall cause the sacrifice and the oblation to cease, and for the overspreading of abominations he shall make it desolate, even until the consummation, and that determined shall be poured upon the desolate."*

† Daniel 12:7, *"And I heard the man clothed in linen, which was upon the waters of the river, when he held up his right hand and his left hand unto heaven, and sware by him that liveth for ever that it shall be for a time, times, and an half; and when he shall have accomplished to scatter the power of the holy people, all these things shall be finished."*

† Revelation 11:2-3, *"²But the court which is without the temple leave out, and measure it not; for it is given unto the Gentiles: and the holy city shall they tread under foot forty and two months. ³And I will give power unto my two witnesses, and they shall prophesy a thousand two hundred and threescore days, clothed in sackcloth."*

† Revelation 12:6, *"And the woman fled into the wilderness, where she hath a place prepared of God, that they should feed her there a thousand two hundred and threescore days."*

† Revelation 12:14, *"And to the woman were given two wings of a great eagle, that she might fly into the wilderness, into her place, where she is nourished for a time, and times, and half a time, from the face of the serpent."*

† Revelation 13:5, *"And there was given unto him a mouth speaking great things and blasphemies; and power was given unto him to continue forty and two months."*

During the Tribulation there will be judgments upon the earth. They are called, seals, trumpets, and bowls (vials) in the scriptures. Each set holds seven judgments. The seven seals are first and next the seven trumpets become more intense, and last the set of seven bowls become the worst. The chart below organizes the scriptures on each set of judgments. The chart reads vertically and horizontally. When read vertically it shows the events of the judgments in sequential order. When read horizontally comparison of the judgment's intensity or worsening state becomes more evident. After which, I have provided another view of the judgments. That chart provides each individual judgment with a few notes or comments to assist you in further study.

THE JUDGMENTS
SEALS, TRUMPETS, BOWLS

Judgment	Seals	Trumpets	Bowls/Vials
1st	**Revelation 6:1-2** And I saw when the Lamb opened one of the seals, and I heard, as it were the noise of thunder, one of the four beasts saying, Come and see. ² And I saw, and behold a white horse: and he that sat on him had a bow; and a crown was given unto him: and he went forth conquering, and to conquer.	**Revelation 8:6-7** ⁶ And the seven angels which had the seven trumpets prepared themselves to sound. ⁷ The first angel sounded, and there followed hail and fire mingled with blood, and they were cast upon the earth: and the third part of trees was burnt up, and all green grass was burnt up.	**Revelation 16:1-2** And I heard a great voice out of the temple saying to the seven angels, Go your ways, and pour out the vials of the wrath of God upon the earth. ² And the first went, and poured out his vial upon the earth; and there fell a noisome and grievous sore upon the men which had the mark of the beast, and upon them which worshipped his image.
2nd	**Revelation 6:3-4** ³ And when he had opened the second seal, I heard the second beast say, Come and see. ⁴ And there went out another horse that was red: and power was given to him that sat thereon to take peace from the earth, and that they should kill one another: and there was given unto him a great sword.	**Revelation 8:8-9** ⁸ And the second angel sounded, and as it were a great mountain burning with fire was cast into the sea: and the third part of the sea became blood; ⁹ And the third part of the creatures which were in the sea, and had life, died; and the third part of the ships were destroyed.	**Revelation 16:3** ³ And the second angel poured out his vial upon the sea; and it became as the blood of a dead man: and every living soul died in the sea.
3rd	**Revelation 6:5-6** ⁵ And when he had opened the third seal, I heard the third beast say, Come and see. And I beheld, and lo a black horse; and he that sat on him had a pair of balances in his hand. ⁶ And I heard a voice in the	**Revelation 8:10-11** ¹⁰ And the third angel sounded, and there fell a great star from heaven, burning as it were a lamp, and it fell upon the third part of the rivers, and upon the fountains of waters;	**Revelation 16:4-7** ⁴ And the third angel poured out his vial upon the rivers and fountains of waters; and they became blood. ⁵ And I heard the angel of the waters say, Thou

	midst of the four beasts say, A measure of wheat for a penny, and three measures of barley for a penny; and see thou hurt not the oil and the wine.	^{11} And the name of the star is called Wormwood: and the third part of the waters became wormwood; and many men died of the waters, because they were made bitter.	art righteous, O Lord, which art, and wast, and shalt be, because thou hast judged thus. ^{6} For they have shed the blood of saints and prophets, and thou hast given them blood to drink; for they are worthy. ^{7} And I heard another out of the altar say, Even so, Lord God Almighty, true and righteous are thy judgments.
4th	**Revelation 6:7-8** ^{7} And when he had opened the fourth seal, I heard the voice of the fourth beast say, Come and see. ^{8} And I looked, and behold a pale horse: and his name that sat on him was Death, and Hell followed with him. And power was given unto them over the fourth part of the earth, to kill with sword, and with hunger, and with death, and with the beasts of the earth.	**Revelation 8:12-13** ^{12} And the fourth angel sounded, and the third part of the sun was smitten, and the third part of the moon, and the third part of the stars; so as the third part of them was darkened, and the day shone not for a third part of it, and the night likewise. ^{13} And I beheld, and heard an angel flying through the midst of heaven, saying with a loud voice, Woe, woe, woe, to the inhabiters of the earth by reason of the other voices of the trumpet of the three angels, which are yet to sound!	**Revelation 16: 8-9** ^{8} And the fourth angel poured out his vial upon the sun; and power was given unto him to scorch men with fire. ^{9} And men were scorched with great heat, and blasphemed the name of God, which hath power over these plagues: and they repented not to give him glory.
5th	**Revelation 6:9-11** ^{9} And when he had opened the fifth seal, I saw under the altar the souls of them that were slain for the word of God, and for the testimony which they held: ^{10} And they cried with a loud	**Revelation 9:1-11** And the fifth angel sounded, and I saw a star fall from heaven unto the earth: and to him was given the key of the bottomless pit. ^{2} And he opened the bottomless pit; and there	**Revelation 16:10-11** ^{10} And the fifth angel poured out his vial upon the seat of the beast; and his kingdom was full of darkness; and they gnawed their tongues for pain,

voice, saying, How long, O Lord, holy and true, dost thou not judge and avenge our blood on them that dwell on the earth?

11 And white robes were given unto every one of them; and it was said unto them, that they should rest yet for a little season, until their fellow servants also and their brethren, that should be killed as they were, should be fulfilled.

arose a smoke out of the pit, as the smoke of a great furnace; and the sun and the air were darkened by reason of the smoke of the pit.

3 And there came out of the smoke locusts upon the earth: and unto them was given power, as the scorpions of the earth have power.

4 And it was commanded them that they should not hurt the grass of the earth, neither any green thing, neither any tree; but only those men which have not the seal of God in their foreheads.

5 And to them it was given that they should not kill them, but that they should be tormented five months: and their torment was as the torment of a scorpion, when he striketh a man.

6 And in those days shall men seek death, and shall not find it; and shall desire to die, and death shall flee from them.

7 And the shapes of the locusts were like unto horses prepared unto battle; and on their heads were as it were crowns like gold, and their faces were as the faces of men.

8 And they had hair as the hair of women, and their teeth were as the teeth of lions.

9 And they had breastplates, as it were breastplates of

11 And blasphemed the God of heaven because of their pains and their sores, and repented not of their deeds.

		iron; and the sound of their wings was as the sound of chariots of many horses running to battle. ¹⁰ And they had tails like unto scorpions, and there were stings in their tails: and their power was to hurt men five months. ¹¹ And they had a king over them, which is the angel of the bottomless pit, whose name in the Hebrew tongue is Abaddon, but in the Greek tongue hath his name Apollyon. ¹² One woe is past; and, behold, there come two woes more hereafter	
6ᵗʰ	**Revelation 6:12-17** ¹² And I beheld when he had opened the sixth seal, and, lo, there was a great earthquake; and the sun became black as sackcloth of hair, and the moon became as blood; ¹³ And the stars of heaven fell unto the earth, even as a fig tree casteth her untimely figs, when she is shaken of a mighty wind. ¹⁴ And the heaven departed as a scroll when it is rolled together; and every mountain and island were moved out of their places. ¹⁵ And the kings of the earth, and the great men, and the rich men, and the chief captains, and the mighty men, and every bondman, and every free man, hid	**Revelation 9:13-21** ¹³ And the sixth angel sounded, and I heard a voice from the four horns of the golden altar which is before God, ¹⁴ Saying to the sixth angel which had the trumpet, Loose the four angels which are bound in the great river Euphrates. ¹⁵ And the four angels were loosed, which were prepared for an hour, and a day, and a month, and a year, for to slay the third part of men. ¹⁶ And the number of the army of the horsemen were two hundred thousand thousand: and I heard the number of them.	**Revelation 16:12-16** ¹² And the sixth angel poured out his vial upon the great river Euphrates; and the water thereof was dried up, that the way of the kings of the east might be prepared. ¹³ And I saw three unclean spirits like frogs come out of the mouth of the dragon, and out of the mouth of the beast, and out of the mouth of the false prophet. ¹⁴ For they are the spirits of devils, working miracles, which go forth unto the kings of the earth and of the whole world, to gather them to the battle of that great day of God Almighty.

	themselves in the dens and in the rocks of the mountains; ¹⁶ And said to the mountains and rocks, Fall on us, and hide us from the face of him that sitteth on the throne, and from the wrath of the Lamb: ¹⁷ For the great day of his wrath is come; and who shall be able to stand?	¹⁷ And thus I saw the horses in the vision, and them that sat on them, having breastplates of fire, and of jacinth, and brimstone: and the heads of the horses were as the heads of lions; and out of their mouths issued fire and smoke and brimstone. ¹⁸ By these three was the third part of men killed, by the fire, and by the smoke, and by the brimstone, which issued out of their mouths. ¹⁹ For their power is in their mouth, and in their tails: for their tails were like unto serpents, and had heads, and with them they do hurt. ²⁰ And the rest of the men which were not killed by these plagues yet repented not of the works of their hands, that they should not worship devils, and idols of gold, and silver, and brass, and stone, and of wood: which neither can see, nor hear, nor walk: ²¹ Neither repented they of their murders, nor of their sorceries, nor of their fornication, nor of their thefts	¹⁵ Behold, I come as a thief. Blessed is he that watcheth, and keepeth his garments, lest he walk naked, and they see his shame. ¹⁶ And he gathered them together into a place called in the Hebrew tongue Armageddon.
7ᵗʰ	**Revelation 8:1-5** And when he had opened the seventh seal, there was silence in heaven about the space of half an hour. ² And I saw the seven angels which stood before God; and	**Revelation 11:15-19** ¹⁵ And the seventh angel sounded; and there were great voices in heaven, saying, The kingdoms of this world are become the kingdoms of our Lord, and of his Christ; and he shall reign for ever and ever.	**Revelation 16:17-21** ¹⁷ And the seventh angel poured out his vial into the air; and there came a great voice out of the temple of heaven, from the throne, saying, It is done.

to them were given seven trumpets.

3 And another angel came and stood at the altar, having a golden censer; and there was given unto him much incense, that he should offer it with the prayers of all saints upon the golden altar which was before the throne.

4 And the smoke of the incense, which came with the prayers of the saints, ascended up before God out of the angel's hand.

5 And the angel took the censer, and filled it with fire of the altar, and cast it into the earth: and there were voices, and thunderings, and lightnings, and an earthquake.

16 And the four and twenty elders, which sat before God on their seats, fell upon their faces, and worshipped God,

17 Saying, We give thee thanks, O LORD God Almighty, which art, and wast, and art to come; because thou hast taken to thee thy great power, and hast reigned.

18 And the nations were angry, and thy wrath is come, and the time of the dead, that they should be judged, and that thou shouldest give reward unto thy servants the prophets, and to the saints, and them that fear thy name, small and great; and shouldest destroy them which destroy the earth.

19 And the temple of God was opened in heaven, and there was seen in his temple the ark of his testament: and there were lightnings, and voices, and thunderings, and an earthquake, and great hail.

18 And there were voices, and thunders, and lightnings; and there was a great earthquake, such as was not since men were upon the earth, so mighty an earthquake, and so great.

19 And the great city was divided into three parts, and the cities of the nations fell: and great Babylon came in remembrance before God, to give unto her the cup of the wine of the fierceness of his wrath.

20 And every island fled away, and the mountains were not found.

21 And there fell upon men a great hail out of heaven, every stone about the weight of a talent: and men blasphemed God because of the plague of the hail; for the plague thereof was exceeding great.

COMMENTS ON THE SEAL JUDGMENTS

#	Seals	Comments
1	Revelation 6:1-2 And I saw when the Lamb opened one of the seals, and I heard, as it were the noise of thunder, one of the four beasts saying, Come and see. ² And I saw, and behold a white horse: and he that sat on him had a bow; and a crown was given unto him: and he went forth conquering, and to conquer.	• The rider is not Christ. Christ appears in Revelation 19:11-21 as a White Horse Rider. Christ appears here as a Lamb and is the one opening the seals. Rider is the Antichrist, imitating Christ. He is not yet revealed as Antichrist until Middle of Tribulation. • Does not say he had an arrow. Rules with bow not sword. Bow means military might. Daniel 8:24, 11:38-39; Second Thessalonians 2:9. • No arrow indicates Antichrist comes as man of peace in the beginning. • Appears uncrowned at first --afterward crowned. Crown given as a gift not as a reward like believers will receive. Crown means power to rule. • Only one weapon--bow.
2	Revelation 6:3-4 ³ And when he had opened the second seal, I heard the second beast say, Come and see. ⁴ And there went out another horse that was red: and power was given to him that sat thereon to take peace from the earth, and that they should kill one another: and there was given unto him a great sword.	• Red symbolizes blood and the sword of war with extraordinary power. • Antichrist has power to remove peace from the earth. • Result of this war may be when Antichrist becomes head of the "Ten Kingdom Federation". Daniel 2:31-35, 40-45; 7:7-8, 19-24; Revelation 13:1-2;17; 3, 7, 12-16. Matthew 24:6-7. • Only one weapon -- large sword.
3	Revelation 6:5-6 ⁵ And when he had opened the third seal, I heard the third beast say, Come and see. And I beheld, and lo a black horse; and he that sat on him had a pair of balances in his hand. ⁶ And I heard a voice in the midst of the four beasts say, A measure of wheat for a penny, and three measures of barley for a penny; and see thou hurt not the oil and the wine.	• Black symbolizes famine, grief and mourning. Pair of balances symbolizes the high cost of food, economic disaster and famine. Men have been called to war and fields go untilled as Christ said in Matthew 24:7. A little wheat will equal a day's wage. • Only two weapons -- economic disaster and famine.
4	Revelation 6:7-8 ⁷ And when he had opened the fourth seal, I heard the voice of the fourth beast say, Come and see. ⁸ And I looked, and behold a pale horse: and his name that sat on him was Death, and Hell	• Pale symbolizes death, spoiled meat and rotten flesh. • Rider looking for those destined to hell. Hell follows death. • Rider has four weapons- sword, famine, plague, and wild beasts. Note the progression of intensity and number of weapons.

	followed with him. And power was given unto them over the fourth part of the earth, to kill with sword, and with hunger, and with death, and with the beasts of the earth.	•	Ezekiel 14:21
5	Revelation 6:9-11 ⁹ And when he had opened the fifth seal, I saw ~~under~~ the altar the souls of them that were slain for the word of God, and for the testimony which they held: ¹⁰ And they cried with a loud voice, saying, How long, O Lord, holy and true, dost thou not judge and avenge our blood on them that dwell on the earth? ¹¹ And white robes were given unto every one of them; and it was said unto them, that they should rest yet for a little season, until their fellow servants also and their brethren, that should be killed as they were, should be fulfilled.	• • •	Those slain for their testimony during Tribulation --called Tribulation saint-- not those who were already resurrected with the Church Rapture. Revelation 12:11 White signifies righteousness of Christ. The Tribulation Saints will rest for a while to wait for other believers to be killed. But fulfillment comes in Revelation 20:4.
6	Revelation 6:12-17 ¹² And I beheld when he had opened the sixth seal, and, lo, there was a great earthquake; and the sun became black as sackcloth of hair, and the moon became as blood; ¹³ And the stars of heaven fell unto the earth, even as a fig tree casteth her untimely figs, when she is shaken of a mighty wind. ¹⁴ And the heaven departed as a scroll when it is rolled together; and every mountain and island were moved out of their places. ¹⁵ And the kings of the earth, and the great men, and the rich men, and the chief captains, and the mighty men, and every bondman, and every free man, hid themselves in the dens and in the rocks of the mountains; ¹⁶ And said to the mountains and rocks, Fall on us, and hide us from the face of him that sitteth on the throne, and from the wrath of the Lamb: ¹⁷ For the great day of his wrath is come; and who shall be able to stand?	• • • • • • •	Great Eathquake (seismos)means a shaking, tempest. Strong's # 4578. The whole earth will shake- convulse when the sixth seal is opened enough to cause the stars of heaven to fall. Perhaps it may be a nuclear explosion or caused by one. Great environmental and physical changes occur, so much that people will call for the mountains and rocks to fall on them. See Isaiah 13:9-11; Ezekiel 29:9-12; 30:3-6; Joel 2:30-31; Matthew 24:29. They should call on Jesus instead of mountains and rocks! Day of His wrath = Tribulation ***Before opening the seventh seal there seems to be a pause. **Read Revelation 7:1-9.** Note: From Revelation 7:1-9... The angel from the east has authority over the other four angels. He holds the seventh seal in his hand. He will mark and seal on the foreheads of **144,000 Jews,** 12,000 from each of the twelve tribes with the "Father's Name" (Revelation 14:1; 22:4). The fullness of the Gentiles will be complete at the

			Rapture (Romans 11:25-27) and the Jews will have special protection from God to evangelize during the Tribulation. Many will be saved. Revelation 7:9
7	Revelation 8:1-5 And when he had opened the seventh seal, there was silence in heaven about the space of half an hour. ² And I saw the seven angels which stood before God; and to them were given seven trumpets. ³ And another angel came and stood at the altar, having a golden censer; and there was given unto him much incense, that he should offer it with the prayers of all saints upon the golden altar which was before the throne. ⁴ And the smoke of the incense, which came with the prayers of the saints, ascended up before God out of the angel's hand. ⁵ And the angel took the censer, and filled it with fire of the altar, and cast it into the earth: and there were voices, and thunderings, and lightnings, and an earthquake.	•	There will be a silence in Heaven for thirty minutes in preparation of worsening events. • The altar of incense represents the prayers of the saints. (Study of Moses' Tabernacle will help --Exodus 25-40).

REFERENCED SCRIPTURES

Seal 1

† Daniel 8:24, *"And his power shall be mighty, but not by his own power: and he shall destroy wonderfully, and shall prosper, and practise, and shall destroy the mighty and the holy people."*

† Daniel 11:38-39, *"³⁸But in his estate shall he honour the God of forces: and a god whom his fathers knew not shall he honour with gold, and silver, and with precious stones, and pleasant things. ³⁹Thus shall he do in the most strong holds with a strange god, whom he shall acknowledge and increase with glory: and he shall cause them to rule over many, and shall divide the land for gain."*

✝ *Second Thessalonians 2:9, "Even him, whose coming is after the working of Satan with all power and signs and lying wonders,"*

✝ *Revelation 19:11-21, "¹¹And I saw heaven opened, and behold a white horse; and he that sat upon him was called Faithful and True, and in righteousness he doth judge and make war. ¹²His eyes were as a flame of fire, and on his head were many crowns; and he had a name written, that no man knew, but he himself. ¹³And he was clothed with a vesture dipped in blood: and his name is called The Word of God. ¹⁴And the armies which were in heaven followed him upon white horses, clothed in fine linen, white and clean. ¹⁵And out of his mouth goeth a sharp sword, that with it he should smite the nations: and he shall rule them with a rod of iron: and he treadeth the winepress of the fierceness and wrath of Almighty God. ¹⁶And he hath on his vesture and on his thigh a name written, KING OF KINGS, AND LORD OF LORDS. ¹⁷And I saw an angel standing in the sun; and he cried with a loud voice, saying to all the fowls that fly in the midst of heaven, Come and gather yourselves together unto the supper of the great God; ¹⁸That ye may eat the flesh of kings, and the flesh of captains, and the flesh of mighty men, and the flesh of horses, and of them that sit on them, and the flesh of all men, both free and bond, both small and great. ¹⁹And I saw the beast, and the kings of the earth, and their armies, gathered together to make war against him that sat on the horse, and against his army. ²⁰And the beast was taken, and with him the false prophet that wrought miracles before him, with which he deceived them that had received the mark of the beast, and them that worshipped his image. These both were cast alive into a lake of fire burning with brimstone. ²¹And the remnant were slain with the sword of him that sat upon the horse, which sword proceeded out of his mouth: and all the fowls were filled with their flesh."*

Seal 2

✝ *Daniel 2:31-35, "³¹Thou, O king, sawest, and behold a great image. This great image, whose brightness was excellent, stood before thee; and the form thereof was terrible. ³²This image's head was of fine* gold, his breast and his arms of silver, his belly and his thighs of brass, *33His legs of iron, his feet part of iron and part of clay. *34Thou sawest till that a stone was cut out without hands, which smote the image upon his feet that were of iron and clay, and brake them to pieces. *35Then was the iron, the clay, the brass, the silver, and the gold, broken to pieces together, and became like the chaff of the summer threshing floors; and the wind carried them away, that no place was found for them: and the stone that smote the image became a great mountain, and filled the whole earth."

† Daniel 2:40-45, "*40And the fourth kingdom shall be strong as iron: forasmuch as iron breaketh in pieces and subdueth all things: and as iron that breaketh all these, shall it break in pieces and bruise. *41And whereas thou sawest the feet and toes, part of potters' clay, and part of iron, the kingdom shall be divided; but there shall be in it of the strength of the iron, forasmuch as thou sawest the iron mixed with miry clay. *42And as the toes of the feet were part of iron, and part of clay, so the kingdom shall be partly strong, and partly broken. *43And whereas thou sawest iron mixed with miry clay, they shall mingle themselves with the seed of men: but they shall not cleave one to another, even as iron is not mixed with clay. *44And in the days of these kings shall the God of heaven set up a kingdom, which shall never be destroyed: and the kingdom shall not be left to other people, but it shall break in pieces and consume all these kingdoms, and it shall stand for ever. *45Forasmuch as thou sawest that the stone was cut out of the mountain without hands, and that it brake in pieces the iron, the brass, the clay, the silver, and the gold; the great God hath made known to the king what shall come to pass hereafter: and the dream is certain, and the interpretation thereof sure."

† Daniel 7:7-8, "*7After this I saw in the night visions, and behold a fourth beast, dreadful and terrible, and strong exceedingly; and it had great iron teeth: it devoured and brake in pieces, and stamped the residue with the feet of it: and it was diverse from all the beasts that were before it; and it had ten horns. *8I considered the horns, and, behold, there came up among them another little horn, before whom there were three of the first horns plucked up by the roots: and, behold,

in this horn were eyes like the eyes of man, and a mouth speaking great things."

† Daniel 7:19-24, *"19Then I would know the truth of the fourth beast, which was diverse from all the others, exceeding dreadful, whose teeth were of iron, and his nails of brass; which devoured, brake in pieces, and stamped the residue with his feet; 20And of the ten horns that were in his head, and of the other which came up, and before whom three fell; even of that horn that had eyes, and a mouth that spake very great things, whose look was more stout than his fellows. 21I beheld, and the same horn made war with the saints, and prevailed against them; 22Until the Ancient of days came, and judgment was given to the saints of the most High; and the time came that the saints possessed the kingdom. 23Thus he said, The fourth beast shall be the fourth kingdom upon earth, which shall be diverse from all kingdoms, and shall devour the whole earth, and shall tread it down, and break it in pieces. 24And the ten horns out of this kingdom are ten kings that shall arise: and another shall rise after them; and he shall be diverse from the first, and he shall subdue three kings."*

† Revelation 13:1-2, *"1And I stood upon the sand of the sea, and saw a beast rise up out of the sea, having seven heads and ten horns, and upon his horns ten crowns, and upon his heads the name of blasphemy. 2And the beast which I saw was like unto a leopard, and his feet were as the feet of a bear, and his mouth as the mouth of a lion: and the dragon gave him his power, and his seat, and great authority."*

† Revelation 17:3, *"So he carried me away in the spirit into the wilderness: and I saw a woman sit upon a scarlet coloured beast, full of names of blasphemy, having seven heads and ten horns."*

† Revelation 17: 7, *"And the angel said unto me, Wherefore didst thou marvel? I will tell thee the mystery of the woman, and of the beast that carrieth her, which hath the seven heads and ten horns."*

† Revelation 17:12-16. *"12And the ten horns which thou sawest are ten kings, which have received no kingdom as yet; but receive power as kings one hour with the beast. 13These have one mind, and shall give*

their power and strength unto the beast. ¹⁴These shall make war with the Lamb, and the Lamb shall overcome them: for he is Lord of lords, and King of kings: and they that are with him are called, and chosen, and faithful. ¹⁵And he saith unto me, The waters which thou sawest, where the whore sitteth, are peoples, and multitudes, and nations, and tongues. ¹⁶And the ten horns which thou sawest upon the beast, these shall hate the whore, and shall make her desolate and naked, and shall eat her flesh, and burn her with fire."

† Matthew 24:6-7, *"⁶And ye shall hear of wars and rumours of wars: see that ye be not troubled: for all these things must come to pass, but the end is not yet. ⁷For nation shall rise against nation, and kingdom against kingdom: and there shall be famines, and pestilences, and earthquakes, in divers places.*

Seal 3

† Matthew 24:7, *"For nation shall rise against nation, and kingdom against kingdom: and there shall be famines, and pestilences, and earthquakes, in divers places."*

Seal 4

† Ezekiel 14:21, *"For thus saith the Lord G*OD*; How much more when I send my four sore judgments upon Jerusalem, the sword, and the famine, and the noisome beast, and the pestilence, to cut off from it man and beast?"*

Seal 5

† Revelation 12:11, *"And they overcame him by the blood of the Lamb, and by the word of their testimony; and they loved not their lives unto the death."*

† Revelation 20:4, *"And I saw thrones, and they sat upon them, and judgment was given unto them: and I saw the souls of them that were beheaded for the witness of Jesus, and for the word of God, and which*

had not worshipped the beast, neither his image, neither had received his mark upon their foreheads, or in their hands; and they lived and reigned with Christ a thousand years."

Seal 6

✝ Isaiah 13:9-11, *"⁹Behold, the day of the* LORD *cometh, cruel both with wrath and fierce anger, to lay the land desolate: and he shall destroy the sinners thereof out of it. ¹⁰For the stars of heaven and the constellations thereof shall not give their light: the sun shall be darkened in his going forth, and the moon shall not cause her light to shine. ¹¹And I will punish the world for their evil, and the wicked for their iniquity; and I will cause the arrogancy of the proud to cease, and will lay low the haughtiness of the terrible."*

✝ Ezekiel 29:9-12, *"⁹And the land of Egypt shall be desolate and waste; and they shall know that I am the* LORD*: because he hath said, The river is mine, and I have made it. ¹⁰Behold, therefore I am against thee, and against thy rivers, and I will make the land of Egypt utterly waste and desolate, from the tower of Syene even unto the border of Ethiopia. ¹¹No foot of man shall pass through it, nor foot of beast shall pass through it, neither shall it be inhabited forty years. ¹²And I will make the land of Egypt desolate in the midst of the countries that are desolate, and her cities among the cities that are laid waste shall be desolate forty years: and I will scatter the Egyptians among the nations, and will disperse them through the countries."*

✝ Ezekiel 30:3-5, *"³For the day is near, even the day of the* LORD *is near, a cloudy day; it shall be the time of the heathen. ⁴And the sword shall come upon Egypt, and great pain shall be in Ethiopia, when the slain shall fall in Egypt, and they shall take away her multitude, and her foundations shall be broken down. ⁵Ethiopia, and Libya, and Lydia, and all the mingled people, and Chub, and the men of the land that is in league, shall fall with them by the sword."*

✝ Joel 2:30-31, *"³⁰And I will shew wonders in the heavens and in the earth, blood, and fire, and pillars of smoke. ³¹The sun shall be turned* into darkness, and the moon into blood, before the great and terrible day of the LORD come."

✝ Matthew 24:29, "Immediately after the tribulation of those days shall the sun be darkened, and the moon shall not give her light, and the stars shall fall from heaven, and the powers of the heavens shall be shaken:"

✝ Romans 11:25-27, "²⁵For I would not, brethren, that ye should be ignorant of this mystery, lest ye should be wise in your own conceits; that blindness in part is happened to Israel, until the fulness of the Gentiles be come in. ²⁶And so all Israel shall be saved: as it is written, There shall come out of Sion the Deliverer, and shall turn away ungodliness from Jacob: ²⁷For this is my covenant unto them, when I shall take away their sins."

✝ Revelation 14:1, "And I looked, and, lo, a Lamb stood on the mount Sion, and with him an hundred forty and four thousand, having his Father's name written in their foreheads."

✝ Revelation 22:4, "And they shall see his face; and his name shall be in their foreheads."

✝ Revelation 7:1-9, "¹And after these things I saw four angels standing on the four corners of the earth, holding the four winds of the earth, that the wind should not blow on the earth, nor on the sea, nor on any tree. ²And I saw another angel ascending from the east, having the seal of the living God: and he cried with a loud voice to the four angels, to whom it was given to hurt the earth and the sea, ³ Saying, Hurt not the earth, neither the sea, nor the trees, till we have sealed the servants of our God in their foreheads. ⁴And I heard the number of them which were sealed: and there were sealed an hundred and forty and four thousand of all the tribes of the children of Israel. ⁵Of the tribe of Juda were sealed twelve thousand. Of the tribe of Reuben were sealed twelve thousand. Of the tribe of Gad were sealed twelve thousand. ⁶Of the tribe of Aser were sealed twelve thousand. Of the tribe of Nephthalim were sealed twelve thousand. Of the tribe of Manasses were sealed twelve thousand. ⁷Of the tribe of Simeon were sealed twelve thousand. Of the tribe of Levi were sealed twelve thousand. Of the tribe of Issachar were sealed twelve thousand. ⁸Of the tribe *of Zabulon were sealed twelve thousand. Of the tribe of Joseph were sealed twelve thousand. Of the tribe of Benjamin were sealed twelve thousand. ⁹After this I beheld, and, lo, a great multitude, which no man could number, of all nations, and kindreds, and people, and tongues, stood before the throne, and before the Lamb, clothed with white robes, and palms in their hands;"*

Seal 7

✝   Study the Tabernacle in Exodus chapters 25-40

COMMENTS ON THE TRUMPET JUDGMENTS

	Trumpets	Comments
1	Revelation 8:6-7 ⁶ And the seven angels which had the seven trumpets prepared themselves to sound. ⁷ The first angel sounded, and there followed hail and fire mingled with blood, and they were cast upon the earth: and the third part of trees was burnt up, and all green grass was burnt up.	• Hail and fire will be mingled with blood and cast upon the earth. One-third of the trees will be burned and all the green grass will be burned. Reminiscent of the seventh plague of Egypt (Exodus 9:22-26). • Fulfillment of Joel 2:30-31.
2	Revelation 8:8-9 ⁸ And the second angel sounded, and as it were a great mountain burning with fire was cast into the sea: and the third part of the sea became blood; ⁹ And the third part of the creatures which were in the sea, and had life, died; and the third part of the ships were destroyed.	• Judgment of the sea
3	Revelation 8:10-11 ¹⁰ And the third angel sounded, and there fell a great star from heaven, burning as it were a lamp, and it fell upon the third part of the rivers, and upon the fountains of waters; ¹¹ And the name of the star is called Wormwood: and the third part of the waters became wormwood; and many men died of the waters, because they were made bitter.	• Great star called Wormwood may be interpreted as a meteor. Maybe an actual star would destroy the whole earth. Angelic beings are sometimes referred to as stars but that doesn't fit here. • Jeremiah 9:13-15; 23:15. • Wormwood means bitter.
4	Revelation 8:12-13 ¹² And the fourth angel sounded, and the third part of the sun was smitten, and the third part of the moon, and the third part of the stars; so as the third part of them was darkened, and the day shone not for a third part of it, and the night likewise. ¹³ And I beheld, and heard an angel flying through the midst of heaven, saying with a loud voice, Woe, woe, woe, to the inhabiters of the earth by reason of the other voices of the trumpet of the three angels, which are yet to sound!	• One-third of the sun, moon and stars are darkened affecting day and night. Luke 21: 25-26. • Three woes proclaimed corresponding to the next three trumpet sounds signifying the worsening of judgments.

5 | Revelation 9:1-11

And the fifth angel sounded, and I saw a star fall from heaven unto the earth: and to him was given the key of the bottomless pit.

² And he opened the bottomless pit; and there arose a smoke out of the pit, as the smoke of a great furnace; and the sun and the air were darkened by reason of the smoke of the pit.

³ And there came out of the smoke locusts upon the earth: and unto them was given power, as the scorpions of the earth have power.

⁴ And it was commanded them that they should not hurt the grass of the earth, neither any green thing, neither any tree; but only those men which have not the seal of God in their foreheads.

⁵ And to them it was given that they should not kill them, but that they should be tormented five months: and their torment was as the torment of a scorpion, when he striketh a man.

⁶ And in those days shall men seek death, and shall not find it; and shall desire to die, and death shall flee from them.

⁷ And the shapes of the locusts were like unto horses prepared unto battle; and on their heads were as it were crowns like gold, and their faces were as the faces of men.

⁸ And they had hair as the hair of women, and their teeth were as the teeth of lions.

⁹ And they had breastplates, as it were breastplates of iron; and the sound of their wings was as the sound of chariots of many horses running to battle.

¹⁰ And they had tails like unto scorpions, and there were stings in their tails: and their power was to hurt men five months.

¹¹ And they had a king over them, which is the angel of the bottomless pit, whose name in the

- This is not a real star and not an astrological body but an angel or person referred to as "him". The star may be Satan but would God give the keys to the pit to Satan? Maybe it is an angel that will eventually cast Satan into the bottomless pit. Maybe it is Wormwood in the previous chapter.
- The pit is opened and the sun and air become dark and powerful locusts are released out of the smoke with specific guidance on what and whom they could hurt.
- People will want to die and they will not be allowed to die.
- First woe. Plague of Locusts.

	Hebrew tongue is Abaddon, but in the Greek tongue hath his name Apollyon.	
	¹² One woe is past; and, behold, there come two woes more hereafter.	
6	Revelation 9:13-21	• The four angels are bound signifying they are "bad" angels. The angels were restrained and prepared for God's exact timing. They are loosed to kill a third part of the people.
	¹³ And the sixth angel sounded, and I heard a voice from the four horns of the golden altar which is before God,	
	¹⁴ Saying to the sixth angel which had the trumpet, Loose the four angels which are bound in the great river Euphrates.	• Military troops will number two hundred thousand thousand (200,000,000). China and possibly India are the only countries possibly big enough. Satan has armies and hierarchical ranks (2 Kings 6:13-17; Ephesians 6:10-18).
	¹⁵ And the four angels were loosed, which were prepared for an hour, and a day, and a month, and a year, for to slay the third part of men.	• Powerful description and yet they don't repent. • A two hundred million-person army! • Second Woe. Plague of Horsemen.
	¹⁶ And the number of the army of the horsemen were two hundred thousand thousand: and I heard the number of them.	• ***Between the sixth and seventh Trumpet there is an interval. **Read Revelation 10-11:14.**
	¹⁷ And thus I saw the horses in the vision, and them that sat on them, having breastplates of fire, and of jacinth, and brimstone: and the heads of the horses were as the heads of lions; and out of their mouths issued fire and smoke and brimstone.	• The mighty angel that comes down from Heaven with the little book may be Christ Jesus because His description is like Revelation 1:12-15. Maybe it is an archangel. Really no one knows. We saw another mighty angel in Revelation 5:2.
	¹⁸ By these three was the third part of men killed, by the fire, and by the smoke, and by the brimstone, which issued out of their mouths.	• Revelation 11: 1-14 gives a description of two witnesses who will prophesy in the last part of the Tribulation. They are believed to be Elijah and Moses. Elijah was the one who shut up heaven that it didn't rain and Moses is the only one who had power to turn water to blood.
	¹⁹ For their power is in their mouth, and in their tails: for their tails were like unto serpents, and had heads, and with them they do hurt.	However, others say John the Baptist. Others say he will be like Elijah in spirit and power. The Two witnesses prophesy 3 ½ years during the Tribulation and
	²⁰ And the rest of the men which were not killed by these plagues yet repented not of the works of their hands, that they should not worship devils, and idols of gold, and silver, and brass, and stone, and of wood: which neither can see, nor hear, nor walk:	will destroy enemies with fire. During the time of their testimony they are supernaturally protected from death but afterwards will be killed by the Antichrist. Their dead bodies will lie in the street for 3 ½ days but they will be resurrected by God's breath and will ascend to heaven in a cloud!
	²¹ Neither repented they of their murders, nor of their sorceries, nor of their fornication, nor of their thefts.	• Even during Tribulation as they are filled with the Holy Spirit (oil and light) fighting the forces of darkness- (Zechariah 4).

		Their bodies will lie in the street where Jesus was crucified (Revelation 11:8).
		• Revelation 11:13 earthquake ends the "Second Woe". 7,000 will die. Others will give God glory.
		• Exodus 7; 1 Kings 17: 1-7; Zechariah 4: 2-6, 4:11-14; Malachi 4:5-6; Acts 1:10-11 Jude 9
7	Revelation 11:15-19 ¹⁵ And the seventh angel sounded; and there were great voices in heaven, saying, The kingdoms of this world are become the kingdoms of our Lord, and of his Christ; and he shall reign for ever and ever. ¹⁶ And the four and twenty elders, which sat before God on their seats, fell upon their faces, and worshipped God, ¹⁷ Saying, We give thee thanks, O LORD God Almighty, which art, and wast, and art to come; because thou hast taken to thee thy great power, and hast reigned. ¹⁸ And the nations were angry, and thy wrath is come, and the time of the dead, that they should be judged, and that thou shouldest give reward unto thy servants the prophets, and to the saints, and them that fear thy name, small and great; and shouldest destroy them which destroy the earth. ¹⁹ And the temple of God was opened in heaven, and there was seen in his temple the ark of his testament: and there were lightnings, and voices, and thunderings, and an earthquake, and great hail.	• Revelation 10:6—no more delays. God's wrath concluding. Zechariah 12 and 14 nations of earth will gather against Jerusalem. • Two wonders appear in Heaven: sun-clothed woman and great red dragon. • The woman is Israel not the Church or Virgin Mary. • Worshipping in Heaven. • Satan knows his time is near and nations unite to stir up war. • **Read Revelation 14-15**. Babylon is today Iraq. Antichrist existed but no one knew who he was. He reveals himself in the middle of the Tribulation or "Middle of the Week". The third angel warns against taking the mark. • Whoever takes the mark of the beast (666), his image or mark of his name will drink the wrath of God. • Note the number of harvests in chapter fourteen.

SCRIPTURES REFERENCED

Trumpet 1

† Exodus 9:22-26, *"²²And the LORD said unto Moses, Stretch forth thine hand toward heaven, that there may be hail in all the land*

of Egypt, upon man, and upon beast, and upon every herb of the field, throughout the land of Egypt. ^{23}And Moses stretched forth his rod toward heaven: and the LORD *sent thunder and hail, and the fire ran along upon the ground; and the* LORD *rained hail upon the land of Egypt. ^{24}So there was hail, and fire mingled with the hail, very grievous, such as there was none like it in all the land of Egypt since it became a nation. ^{25}And the hail smote throughout all the land of Egypt all that was in the field, both man and beast; and the hail smote every herb of the field, and brake every tree of the field. ^{26}Only in the land of Goshen, where the children of Israel were, was there no hail."*

† Joel 2:30-31, *"^{30}And I will shew wonders in the heavens and in the earth, blood, and fire, and pillars of smoke. ^{31}The sun shall be turned into darkness, and the moon into blood, before the great and terrible day of the* LORD *come."*

Trumpet 2

† None

Trumpet 3

† Jeremiah 9:13-15, *"^{13}And the* LORD *saith, Because they have forsaken my law which I set before them, and have not obeyed my voice, neither walked therein; ^{14}But have walked after the imagination of their own heart, and after Baalim, which their fathers taught them: ^{15}Therefore thus saith the* LORD *of hosts, the God of Israel; Behold, I will feed them, even this people, with wormwood, and give them water of gall to drink."*

† Jeremiah 23:15, *"Therefore thus saith the* LORD *of hosts concerning the prophets; Behold, I will feed them with wormwood, and make them drink the water of gall: for from the prophets of Jerusalem is profaneness gone forth into all the land."*

Trumpet 4

† Luke 21:25-26, *"²⁵And there shall be signs in the sun, and in the moon, and in the stars; and upon the earth distress of nations, with perplexity; the sea and the waves roaring; ²⁶Men's hearts failing them for fear, and for looking after those things which are coming on the earth: for the powers of heaven shall be shaken."*

Trumpet 5

† None

Trumpet 6

† Exodus 7:1, *"And the L*ORD *said unto Moses, See, I have made thee a god to Pharaoh: and Aaron thy brother shall be thy prophet."*

† First Kings 17:1-7, *"¹And Elijah the Tishbite, who was of the inhabitants of Gilead, said unto Ahab, As the L*ORD *God of Israel liveth, before whom I stand, there shall not be dew nor rain these years, but according to my word. ²And the word of the L*ORD *came unto him, saying, ³Get thee hence, and turn thee eastward, and hide thyself by the brook Cherith, that is before Jordan. ⁴And it shall be, that thou shalt drink of the brook; and I have commanded the ravens to feed thee there. ⁵So he went and did according unto the word of the L*ORD*: for he went and dwelt by the brook Cherith, that is before Jordan. ⁶And the ravens brought him bread and flesh in the morning, and bread and flesh in the evening; and he drank of the brook. ⁷And it came to pass after a while, that the brook dried up, because there had been no rain in the land."*

† Second Kings 6:13-17, *"¹³And he said, Go and spy where he is, that I may send and fetch him. And it was told him, saying, Behold, he is in Dothan. ¹⁴Therefore sent he thither horses, and chariots, and a great host: and they came by night, and compassed the city about. ¹⁵And when the servant of the man of God was risen early, and gone forth, behold, an host compassed the city both with horses and chariots. And his servant said unto him, Alas, my master! how shall we do? ¹⁶And he answered, Fear not: for they that be with us are more than they that be with them.¹⁷And Elisha prayed, and said, L*ORD*, I pray thee, open*

his eyes, that he may see. And the LORD opened the eyes of the young man; and he saw: and, behold, the mountain was full of horses and chariots of fire round about Elisha."

✝ Read Zechariah 4

✝ Zechariah 4:2-6, *"²And said unto me, What seest thou? And I said, I have looked, and behold a candlestick all of gold, with a bowl upon the top of it, and his seven lamps thereon, and seven pipes to the seven lamps, which are upon the top thereof: ³And two olive trees by it, one upon the right side of the bowl, and the other upon the left side thereof. ⁴So I answered and spake to the angel that talked with me, saying, What are these, my lord? ⁵Then the angel that talked with me answered and said unto me, Knowest thou not what these be? And I said, No, my lord. ⁶Then he answered and spake unto me, saying, This is the word of the LORD unto Zerubbabel, saying, Not by might, nor by power, but by my spirit, saith the LORD of hosts."*

✝ Zechariah 4:11-14, *"¹¹Then answered I, and said unto him, What are these two olive trees upon the right side of the candlestick and upon the left side thereof? ¹²And I answered again, and said unto him, What be these two olive branches which through the two golden pipes empty the golden oil out of themselves? ¹³And he answered me and said, Knowest thou not what these be? And I said, No, my lord. ¹⁴Then said he, These are the two anointed ones, that stand by the LORD of the whole earth."*

✝ Malachi 4:5-6, *"⁵Behold, I will send you Elijah the prophet before the coming of the great and dreadful day of the LORD: ⁶And he shall turn the heart of the fathers to the children, and the heart of the children to their fathers, lest I come and smite the earth with a curse."*

✝ Acts 1:10-11, *"¹⁰And while they looked stedfastly toward heaven as he went up, behold, two men stood by them in white apparel; ¹¹Which also said, Ye men of Galilee, why stand ye gazing up into heaven? this same Jesus, which is taken up from you into heaven, shall so come in like manner as ye have seen him go into heaven."*

✝ Ephesians 6: 10-18, *"¹⁰Finally, my brethren, be strong in the Lord, and in the power of his might. ¹¹Put on the whole armour of God, that ye may be able to stand against the wiles of the devil. ¹²For we wrestle not against flesh and blood, but against principalities, against powers, against the rulers of the darkness of this world, against spiritual wickedness in high places. ¹³Wherefore take unto you the whole armour of God, that ye may be able to withstand in the evil day, and having done all, to stand. ¹⁴Stand therefore, having your loins girt about with truth, and having on the breastplate of righteousness; ¹⁵And your feet shod with the preparation of the gospel of peace; ¹⁶Above all, taking the shield of faith, wherewith ye shall be able to quench all the fiery darts of the wicked. ¹⁷And take the helmet of salvation, and the sword of the Spirit, which is the word of God: ¹⁸Praying always with all prayer and supplication in the Spirit, and watching thereunto with all perseverance and supplication for all saints;"*

† Jude 1:9, *"Yet Michael the archangel, when contending with the devil he disputed about the body of Moses, durst not bring against him a railing accusation, but said, The Lord rebuke thee."*

† Revelation 1:12-15, *"¹²And I turned to see the voice that spake with me. And being turned, I saw seven golden candlesticks; ¹³And in the midst of the seven candlesticks one like unto the Son of man, clothed with a garment down to the foot, and girt about the paps with a golden girdle. ¹⁴His head and his hairs were white like wool, as white as snow; and his eyes were as a flame of fire; ¹⁵And his feet like unto fine brass, as if they burned in a furnace; and his voice as the sound of many waters."*

† Revelation 5:2, *"And I saw a strong angel proclaiming with a loud voice, Who is worthy to open the book, and to loose the seals thereof?"*

† Read Revelation 10-11:14

† Revelation 11:1-14, *"¹And there was given me a reed like unto a rod: and the angel stood, saying, Rise, and measure the temple of God, and the altar, and them that worship therein. ²But the court which is without the temple leave out, and measure it not; for it is given unto the Gentiles: and the holy city shall they tread under foot forty and two months. ³And I will give power unto my two witnesses, and they shall prophesy a thousand two hundred and threescore days, clothed in sackcloth. ⁴These are the two olive trees,*

and the two candlesticks standing before the God of the earth. ⁵And if any man will hurt them, fire proceedeth out of their mouth, and devoureth their enemies: and if any man will hurt them, he must in this manner be killed. ⁶These have power to shut heaven, that it rain not in the days of their prophecy: and have power over waters to turn them to blood, and to smite the earth with all plagues, as often as they will. ⁷And when they shall have finished their testimony, the beast that ascendeth out of the bottomless pit shall make war against them, and shall overcome them, and kill them. ⁸And their dead bodies shall lie in the street of the great city, which spiritually is called Sodom and Egypt, where also our Lord was crucified. ⁹And they of the people and kindreds and tongues and nations shall see their dead bodies three days and an half, and shall not suffer their dead bodies to be put in graves. ¹⁰And they that dwell upon the earth shall rejoice over them, and make merry, and shall send gifts one to another; because these two prophets tormented them that dwelt on the earth. ¹¹And after three days and an half the spirit of life from God entered into them, and they stood upon their feet; and great fear fell upon them which saw them. ¹²And they heard a great voice from heaven saying unto them, Come up hither. And they ascended up to heaven in a cloud; and their enemies beheld them. ¹³And the same hour was there a great earthquake, and the tenth part of the city fell, and in the earthquake were slain of men seven thousand: and the remnant were affrighted, and gave glory to the God of heaven. ¹⁴The second woe is past; and, behold, the third woe cometh quickly."

Trumpet 7

- † Read Zechariah 12 and 14
- † Revelation 10:6, *"And sware by him that liveth for ever and ever, who created heaven, and the things that therein are, and the earth, and the things that therein are, and the sea, and the things which are therein, that there should be time no longer:"*
- † Read Revelation 14 and 15

COMMENTS ON BOWL/VIAL JUDGMENTS

#	Bowls/Vials	Comments
1	Revelation 16:1-2 And I heard a great voice out of the temple saying to the seven angels, Go your ways, and pour out the vials of the wrath of God upon the earth. ² And the first went, and poured out his vial upon the earth; and there fell a noisome and grievous sore upon the men which had the mark of the beast, and upon them which worshipped his image.	• Those who take the mark of the beast will have horrible sores, which will be very painful, and smell awful. • Compare with the sixth plague of Egypt Exodus 9: 8-12.
2	Revelation 16:3 ³ And the second angel poured out his vial upon the sea; and it became as the blood of a dead man: and every living soul died in the sea.	• Sea is turned into blood and everything is killed in the sea. Compare with second trumpet. Vials are worse.
3	Revelation 16:4-7 ⁴ And the third angel poured out his vial upon the rivers and fountains of waters; and they became blood. ⁵ And I heard the angel of the waters say, Thou art righteous, O Lord, which art, and wast, and shalt be, because thou hast judged thus. ⁶ For they have shed the blood of saints and prophets, and thou hast given them blood to drink; for they are worthy. ⁷ And I heard another out of the altar say, Even so, Lord God Almighty, true and righteous are thy judgments.	• Rivers and streams become blood. Compare to the third trumpet and also to the first Egyptian plague (Exodus 7:19-24). Only blood to drink for the thirsty.
4	Revelation 16: 8-9 ⁸ And the fourth angel poured out his vial upon the sun; and power was given unto him to scorch men with fire. ⁹ And men were scorched with great heat, and blasphemed the name of God, which hath power over these plagues: and they repented not to give him glory.	• Great heat scorches upon people. They blasphemed the Name of God! They still don't repent. (Malachi 4:1) • This vial has no parallel in the Egyptian plagues - the only one that doesn't have the parallel.

5	Revelation 16:10-11	• Darkness over all the kingdom of the beast and great pain causing people to gnaw their tongues.
	[10] And the fifth angel poured out his vial upon the seat of the beast; and his kingdom was full of darkness; and they gnawed their tongues for pain,	• Compare Ninth Egyptian plague (Exodus 10: 21-23).
		• Think about darkness that covered the earth when Jesus hung on cross (Matthew 27: 45; Luke 23: 44-45)
	[11] And blasphemed the God of heaven because of their pains and their sores, and repented not of their deeds.	• Joel 2:1-3, 31 describes darkness.
6	Revelation 16:12-16	• Euphrates dried up so the nations, Kings of the East can cross over to gather for Battle of Armageddon. Compare to the opening of the Red Sea (Exodus 14:21; Isaiah 11: 15-16).
	[12] And the sixth angel poured out his vial upon the great river Euphrates; and the water thereof was dried up, that the way of the kings of the east might be prepared.	
		• Dragon = Anti-God, Beast = Antichrist, False Prophet = Anti-Holy Spirit called the unholy trinity or the Satanic trinity. Satan always tries to mimic God.
	[13] And I saw three unclean spirits like frogs come out of the mouth of the dragon, and out of the mouth of the beast, and out of the mouth of the false prophet.	• Compare second plague of Egypt (Exodus 8: 1-2).
		• Spirits- First Kings 22: 20-38; Matthew 24: 24-25; Second Thessalonians 2:9; First Timothy 4:1.
	[14] For they are the spirits of devils, working miracles, which go forth unto the kings of the earth and of the whole world, to gather them to the battle of that great day of God Almighty.	• Will come unexpectedly as a thief. Surprise!
	[15] Behold, I come as a thief. Blessed is he that watcheth, and keepeth his garments, lest he walk naked, and they see his shame.	• Only time Armageddon mentioned in Bible. Two hundred million-person army will fight from the East (China, India, and armies from all over the world).
	[16] And he gathered them together into a place called in the Hebrew tongue Armageddon.	
7	Revelation 16:17-21	• Jesus cried out from the cross, "It is finished". Great earthquake divides the "Great City" into three parts (Zechariah 14: 4-5).
	[17] And the seventh angel poured out his vial into the air; and there came a great voice out of the temple of heaven, from the throne, saying, It is done.	• Great hail will weigh one- hundred pounds each. Compare Egyptian plague seven in Exodus 9: 13-35; Joshua 10:11
	[18] And there were voices, and thunders, and lightnings; and there was a great earthquake, such as was not since men were upon the earth, so mighty an earthquake, and so great.	• Levitical law commanded death by stoning on those who blaspheme. Here we see hail (stones) from heaven. Leviticus 24:16.
	[19] And the great city was divided into three parts, and the cities of the nations fell: and great Babylon came in remembrance before	• The seventh vial ends the Tribulation but sometime before the end of the Tribulation the Battle of Armageddon begins.

God, to give unto her the cup of the wine of the fierceness of his wrath.

²⁰ And every island fled away, and the mountains were not found.

²¹ And there fell upon men a great hail out of heaven, every stone about the weight of a talent: and men blasphemed God because of the plague of the hail; for the plague thereof was exceeding great.

REFERENCED SCRIPTURES

Bowl 1

✝ Exodus 9:8-12, "*⁸And the* L<small>ORD</small> *said unto Moses and unto Aaron, Take to you handfuls of ashes of the furnace, and let Moses sprinkle it toward the heaven in the sight of Pharaoh. ⁹And it shall become small dust in all the land of Egypt, and shall be a boil breaking forth with blains upon man, and upon beast, throughout all the land of Egypt. ¹⁰And they took ashes of the furnace, and stood before Pharaoh; and Moses sprinkled it up toward heaven; and it became a boil breaking forth with blains upon man, and upon beast. ¹¹And the magicians could not stand before Moses because of the boils; for the boil was upon the magicians, and upon all the Egyptians. ¹²And the* L<small>ORD</small> *hardened the heart of Pharaoh, and he hearkened not unto them; as the* L<small>ORD</small> *had spoken unto Moses.*"

Bowl 2

✝ None

Bowl 3

✝ Exodus 7:19-24, "*¹⁹And the* L<small>ORD</small> *spake unto Moses, Say unto Aaron, Take thy rod, and stretch out thine hand upon the waters of Egypt, upon their streams, upon their rivers, and upon their ponds, and* upon all their pools of water, that they may become blood; and that there may be blood throughout all the land of Egypt, both in vessels of wood, and in vessels of stone. ²⁰And Moses and Aaron did so, as the LORD commanded; and he lifted up the rod, and smote the waters that were in the river, in the sight of Pharaoh, and in the sight of his servants; and all the waters that were in the river were turned to blood. ²¹And the fish that was in the river died; and the river stank, and the Egyptians could not drink of the water of the river; and there was blood throughout all the land of Egypt. ²²And the magicians of Egypt did so with their enchantments: and Pharaoh's heart was hardened, neither did he hearken unto them; as the LORD had said. ²³And Pharaoh turned and went into his house, neither did he set his heart to this also. ²⁴And all the Egyptians digged round about the river for water to drink; for they could not drink of the water of the river."

Bowl 4

† Malachi 4:1, "For, behold, the day cometh, that shall burn as an oven; and all the proud, yea, and all that do wickedly, shall be stubble: and the day that cometh shall burn them up, saith the LORD of hosts, that it shall leave them neither root nor branch."

Bowl 5

† Exodus 10:21-23, "²¹And the LORD said unto Moses, Stretch out thine hand toward heaven, that there may be darkness over the land of Egypt, even darkness which may be felt. ²²And Moses stretched forth his hand toward heaven; and there was a thick darkness in all the land of Egypt three days: ²³They saw not one another, neither rose any from his place for three days: but all the children of Israel had light in their dwellings."

† Joel 2:1-3, "¹Blow ye the trumpet in Zion, and sound an alarm in my holy mountain: let all the inhabitants of the land tremble: for the day of the LORD cometh, for it is nigh at hand; ²A day of darkness and of gloominess, a day of clouds and of thick darkness, as the morning spread upon the mountains: a great people and a strong; there hath not been ever the like, neither shall be any more after it, even to the years of many generations. *³A fire devoureth before them; and behind them a flame burneth: the land is as the garden of Eden before them, and behind them a desolate wilderness; yea, and nothing shall escape them."*

† Joel 2:31, *"The sun shall be turned into darkness, and the moon into blood, before the great and terrible day of the LORD come."*

† Matthew 27:45, *"Now from the sixth hour there was darkness over all the land unto the ninth hour."*

† Luke 23:44-45, *"⁴⁴And it was about the sixth hour, and there was a darkness over all the earth until the ninth hour. ⁴⁵And the sun was darkened, and the veil of the temple was rent in the midst."*

Bowl 6

† Exodus 8:1-2, *"¹And the LORD spake unto Moses, Go unto Pharaoh, and say unto him, Thus saith the LORD, Let my people go, that they may serve me. ²And if thou refuse to let them go, behold, I will smite all thy borders with frogs:"*

† Exodus 14:21, *"And Moses stretched out his hand over the sea; and the LORD caused the sea to go back by a strong east wind all that night, and made the sea dry land, and the waters were divided."*

† First Kings 22:20-38, *"²⁰And the LORD said, Who shall persuade Ahab, that he may go up and fall at Ramothgilead? And one said on this manner, and another said on that manner. ²¹And there came forth a spirit, and stood before the LORD, and said, I will persuade him. ²²And the LORD said unto him, Wherewith? And he said, I will go forth, and I will be a lying spirit in the mouth of all his prophets. And he said, Thou shalt persuade him, and prevail also: go forth, and do so. ²³Now therefore, behold, the LORD hath put a lying spirit in the mouth of all these thy prophets, and the LORD hath spoken evil concerning thee. ²⁴But Zedekiah the son of Chenaanah went near, and smote Micaiah on the cheek, and said, Which way went the Spirit of the LORD from me to speak unto thee? ²⁵And Micaiah said, Behold, thou shalt see in that day, when thou shalt go into an inner chamber to hide thyself. ²⁶And*

the king of Israel said, Take Micaiah, and carry him back unto Amon the governor of the city, and to Joash the king's son; [27]And say, Thus saith the king, Put this fellow in the prison, and feed him with bread of affliction and with water of affliction, until I come in peace. [28]And Micaiah said, If thou return at all in peace, the LORD hath not spoken by me. And he said, Hearken, O people, every one of you. [29]So the king of Israel and Jehoshaphat the king of Judah went up to Ramothgilead. [30]And the king of Israel said unto Jehoshaphat, I will disguise myself, and enter into the battle; but put thou on thy robes. And the king of Israel disguised himself, and went into the battle. [31]But the king of Syria commanded his thirty and two captains that had rule over his chariots, saying, Fight neither with small nor great, save only with the king of Israel. [32]And it came to pass, when the captains of the chariots saw Jehoshaphat, that they said, Surely it is the king of Israel. And they turned aside to fight against him: and Jehoshaphat cried out. [33]And it came to pass, when the captains of the chariots perceived that it was not the king of Israel, that they turned back from pursuing him. [34]And a certain man drew a bow at a venture, and smote the king of Israel between the joints of the harness: wherefore he said unto the driver of his chariot, Turn thine hand, and carry me out of the host; for I am wounded. [35]And the battle increased that day: and the king was stayed up in his chariot against the Syrians, and died at even: and the blood ran out of the wound into the midst of the chariot. [36]And there went a proclamation throughout the host about the going down of the sun, saying, Every man to his city, and every man to his own country. [37]So the king died, and was brought to Samaria; and they buried the king in Samaria. [38]And one washed the chariot in the pool of Samaria; and the dogs licked up his blood; and they washed his armour; according unto the word of the LORD which he spake."

† Isaiah 11:15-16, "[15]And the LORD shall utterly destroy the tongue of the Egyptian sea; and with his mighty wind shall he shake his hand over the river, and shall smite it in the seven streams, and make men go over dryshod. [16]And there shall be an highway for the remnant of his people, which shall be left, from Assyria; like as it was to Israel in the day that he came up out of the land of Egypt."

✝ Matthew 24:24-25, *"²⁴For there shall arise false Christs, and false prophets, and shall shew great signs and wonders; insomuch that, if it were possible, they shall deceive the very elect. ²⁵Behold, I have told you before."*

✝ Second Thessalonians 2:9, *"Even him, whose coming is after the working of Satan with all power and signs and lying wonders,"*

✝ First Timothy 4:1, *"Now the Spirit speaketh expressly, that in the latter times some shall depart from the faith, giving heed to seducing spirits, and doctrines of devils;"*

Bowl 7

✝ Exodus 9:13-35, *"¹³ And the Lord said unto Moses, Rise up early in the morning, and stand before Pharaoh, and say unto him, Thus saith the Lord God of the Hebrews, Let my people go, that they may serve me. ¹⁴For I will at this time send all my plagues upon thine heart, and upon thy servants, and upon thy people; that thou mayest know that there is none like me in all the earth. ¹⁵For now I will stretch out my hand, that I may smite thee and thy people with pestilence; and thou shalt be cut off from the earth. ¹⁶And in very deed for this cause have I raised thee up, for to shew in thee my power; and that my name may be declared throughout all the earth. ¹⁷As yet exaltest thou thyself against my people, that thou wilt not let them go? ¹⁸Behold, to morrow about this time I will cause it to rain a very grievous hail, such as hath not been in Egypt since the foundation thereof even until now. ¹⁹Send therefore now, and gather thy cattle, and all that thou hast in the field; for upon every man and beast which shall be found in the field, and shall not be brought home, the hail shall come down upon them, and they shall die. ²⁰He that feared the word of the Lord among the servants of Pharaoh made his servants and his cattle flee into the houses: ²¹And he that regarded not the word of the Lord left his servants and his cattle in the field. ²²And the Lord said unto Moses, Stretch forth thine hand toward heaven, that there may be hail in all the land of Egypt, upon man, and upon beast, and upon every herb of the field, throughout the land of Egypt. ²³And Moses stretched forth* his rod toward heaven: and the LORD sent thunder and hail, and the fire ran along upon the ground; and the LORD rained hail upon the land of Egypt. ²⁴So there was hail, and fire mingled with the hail, very grievous, such as there was none like it in all the land of Egypt since it became a nation. ²⁵And the hail smote throughout all the land of Egypt all that was in the field, both man and beast; and the hail smote every herb of the field, and brake every tree of the field. ²⁶Only in the land of Goshen, where the children of Israel were, was there no hail. ²⁷And Pharaoh sent, and called for Moses and Aaron, and said unto them, I have sinned this time: the LORD is righteous, and I and my people are wicked. ²⁸Intreat the LORD (for it is enough) that there be no more mighty thunderings and hail; and I will let you go, and ye shall stay no longer. ²⁹And Moses said unto him, As soon as I am gone out of the city, I will spread abroad my hands unto the LORD; and the thunder shall cease, neither shall there be any more hail; that thou mayest know how that the earth is the LORD's. ³⁰But as for thee and thy servants, I know that ye will not yet fear the LORD God. ³¹And the flax and the barley was smitten: for the barley was in the ear, and the flax was bolled. ³²But the wheat and the rie were not smitten: for they were not grown up. ³³And Moses went out of the city from Pharaoh, and spread abroad his hands unto the LORD: and the thunders and hail ceased, and the rain was not poured upon the earth. ³⁴And when Pharaoh saw that the rain and the hail and the thunders were ceased, he sinned yet more, and hardened his heart, he and his servants. ³⁵And the heart of Pharaoh was hardened, neither would he let the children of Israel go; as the LORD had spoken by Moses."

† Levitcus 24:16, "And he that blasphemeth the name of the LORD, he shall surely be put to death, and all the congregation shall certainly stone him: as well the stranger, as he that is born in the land, when he blasphemeth the name of the Lord, shall be put to death."

† Joshua 10:11, "And it came to pass, as they fled from before Israel, and were in the going down to Bethhoron, that the LORD cast down great stones from heaven upon them unto Azekah, and they died: they were more which died with hailstones than they whom the children of Israel slew with the sword."

† Zechariah 14: 4-5, "*And his feet shall stand in that day upon the mount of Olives, which is before Jerusalem on the east, and the mount of Olives shall cleave in the midst thereof toward the east and toward the west, and there shall be a very great valley; and half of the mountain shall remove toward the north, and half of it toward the south. *And ye shall flee to the valley of the mountains; for the valley of the mountains shall reach unto Azal: yea, ye shall flee, like as ye fled from before the earthquake in the days of Uzziah king of Judah: and the LORD my God shall come, and all the saints with thee.*"

RECOMMENDED ACTIVITIES

1. Look up and study various charts on the Internet for Seventy Weeks. Simply write "Daniel Seventy Weeks images" or "chart of Daniel's Seventy Weeks" into the browser and many charts and explanations will pop up. Find one that makes it easy for you to understand and then share with someone that may not have your understanding.

2. Study the Tabernacle of Moses and the Temple more fully.

3. Study the "Times of the Gentiles" and "The Fullness of the Gentiles". It is a simple concept but is highly complicated when studied. Try using this online source to begin. https://www.blueletterbible.org/study/larkin/dt/10.cfm. Afterwards search other reputable sources, which are less detailed, by searching for the difference between the two. Read as many reliable commentators as possible. Make a chart that will help you remember.

Criteria	Fullness of the Gentiles	Times of the Gentiles
Scripture	**Romans 11:25-27**	**Luke 21:24**
Began and End	Began day of Pentecost Ends at the Rapture	Began at the Babylonian Captivity Ends at the Second Coming
Differentiating factor	Numerically, referring to when the last person becomes part of the Church before she is raptured. The time of the Church when she was born to when she will be raptured.	From the time Israel politically came under domination of the Gentile rule.

4. Study the chapters (7, 10, 11. 12. 13, 14, 15) in between the events of the Seals, Trumpets, and Bowls/Vials.
5. Look up this website and learn more about the Jewish months. https://www.chabad.org/library/article_cdo/aid/526874/jewish/The-Jewish-Month.htm

PERSONAL NOTES

CHAPTER TEN

THE UNHOLY TRINITY

Revelation 16:13
And I saw three unclean spirits like frogs come
out of the mouth of the dragon,
and out of the mouth of the beast,
and out of the mouth of the false prophet.

UNHOLY TRINITY

Satan tries to mimic, imitate, and counterfeit the Holy Trinity in the end times as he does always throughout Scripture. He is a sham, a fake, a mockery, bogus, hoax, and a phony! This imitation is called the unholy trinity or satanic trinity. The unholy trinity is comprised of the Dragon, the Beast, and the False Prophet. The Dragon is Satan, the Anti-God, the Beast is the Antichrist, and the False Prophet is the Anti-Holy Spirit or counterfeit Holy Spirit.

DRAGON

Satan is described as the serpent, an angel of light but he is referred to as the great red dragon in Revelation 12:3. He will direct people to worship the Antichrist at the middle of the Tribulation.

Revelation 12:3, *"And there appeared another wonder in heaven; and behold a great red dragon, having seven heads and ten horns, and seven crowns upon his heads."*

Satan mimics in several ways but here are a few of his meager attempts. Satan mimics the Church. The Antichrist worship center will be called the "Synagogue of Satan"

Revelation 2:9, *"I know thy works, and tribulation, and poverty, (but thou art rich) and I know the blasphemy of them which say they are Jews, and are not, but are the synagogue of Satan."*

Revelation 3:9, *"Behold, I will make them of the synagogue of Satan, which say they are Jews, and are not, but do lie; behold, I will make them to come and worship before thy feet, and to know that I have loved thee."*

The Church is considered to be the bride of Christ but Satan's bride is called "MYSTERY, BABYLON THE GREAT, THE MOTHER OF HARLOTS, AND ABOMINATIONS OF THE EARTH".

> ✝ Revelation 17:5, *"And upon her forehead was a name written, MYSTERY, BABYLON THE GREAT, THE MOTHER OF HARLOTS AND ABOMINATIONS OF THE EARTH.*

Christians use a communion cup and the Lord's Table while Satan mimics with a cup of demons and a table of demons.

> ✝ First Corinthians 10: 21, *"Ye cannot drink the cup of the Lord, and the cup of devils: ye cannot be partakers of the Lord's table, and of the table of devils."*

✝ The ministry of Jesus was for three- and one-half years. Satan will "reign" as the Antichrist for three- and one-half years. The actual "reign" of the Antichrist is for forty-two months, which begins after he is revealed at the Middle of the Tribulation.

✝ Revelation 11:1-2, *"¹And there was given me a reed like unto a rod: and the angel stood, saying, Rise, and measure the temple of God, and the altar, and them that worship therein. ²But the court which is without the temple leave out, and measure it not; for it is given unto the Gentiles: and the holy city shall they tread under foot forty and two months."*

ANTICHRIST

The Antichrist, as a political ruler, attempts to bring peace at the beginning of the Tribulation but people do not realize and recognize him as the Antichrist until the middle of the Tribulation. First and Second John, Revelation 12, 13 and Daniel 7, 11 give details on Antichrist.

He will reveal himself at the middle of the Tribulation. He will come out of the sea possibly the Mediterranean Sea. The Dragon (Satan) will give power to the Beast (Antichrist). The Dragon and the Beast are related but different. They differ on their number of crowns. Notice the Dragon has seven heads, ten horns and seven crowns. The Beast has seven heads, ten horns, but has ten crowns. The ten horns represent rulers who will govern with the Antichrist. The seven heads are the seven world governments known also as seven hills or seven mountains. Six of the world governments were Assyrian Empire, Egyptian Empire, Babylonian Empire, Medo-Persian Empire, Greek and Roman Empires. The seventh world government will be controlled by the Antichrist and is thought to be the United Nations. The ten crowns represent ten divisions apportioned by seventh world government. The Beast, The World Government, and the Antichrist are spoken of as the same.

† Revelation 13: 1-18, *"¹And I stood upon the sand of the sea, and saw a beast rise up out of the sea, having seven heads and ten horns, and upon his horns ten crowns, and upon his heads the name of blasphemy. ²And the beast which I saw was like unto a leopard, and his feet were as the feet of a bear, and his mouth as the mouth of a lion: and the dragon gave him his power, and his seat, and great authority. ³And I saw one of his heads as it were wounded to death; and his deadly wound was healed: and all the world wondered after the beast. ⁴And they worshipped the dragon which gave power unto the beast: and they worshipped the beast, saying, Who is like unto the beast? who is able to make war with him? ⁵And there was given unto him a mouth speaking great things and blasphemies; and power was given unto him to continue forty and two months. ⁶And he opened his mouth in blasphemy against God, to blaspheme his name, and his tabernacle, and them that dwell in heaven. ⁷And it was given unto him to make war with the saints, and to overcome them: and power was given him over all kindreds, and tongues, and nations. ⁸And all that dwell upon the earth shall worship him, whose names are not written in the book of life of the Lamb slain from the foundation of the world. ⁹If any man have an ear, let him hear. ¹⁰He that leadeth into captivity shall go into captivity: he that killeth with the sword must be killed with the sword. Here is the patience and the faith of the saints. ¹¹And I beheld another beast coming up out of the earth; and he had two horns like a lamb, and he spake as a dragon. ¹²And he exerciseth all the power of the first beast before him, and causeth the earth and them which dwell therein to worship the first beast, whose deadly wound was healed. ¹³And he doeth great wonders, so that he maketh fire come down from heaven on the earth in the sight of men, ¹⁴And deceiveth them that dwell on the earth by the means of those miracles which he had power to do in the sight of the beast; saying to them that dwell on the earth, that they should make an image to the beast, which had the wound by a sword, and did live. ¹⁵And he had power to give life unto the image of the beast, that the image of the beast should both speak, and cause that as many as would not worship the image of the beast should be killed. ¹⁶And he causeth all, both small and*

great, rich and poor, free and bond, to receive a mark in their right
hand, or in their foreheads: [17]And that no man might buy or sell, save
he that had the mark, or the name of the beast, or the number of his
name. [18]Here is wisdom. Let him that hath understanding count the
number of the beast: for it is the number of a man; and his number is
Six hundred threescore and six."

The Antichrist will attempt to mimic the resurrection of Christ. The
Antichrist will die after a mortal wound and Satan will miraculously
heal him about mid-Tribulation. After which the people begin to
worship Satan and the Antichrist.

✝   Revelation 13:3, "And I saw one of his heads as it were wounded to
    death; and his deadly wound was healed: and all the world wondered
    after the beast."
✝   Revelation 13:4-5, "And they worshipped the dragon which gave
    power unto the beast: and they worshipped the beast, saying, Who
    is like unto the beast? who is able to make war with him? [5]And there
    was given unto him a mouth speaking great things and blasphemies;
    and power was given unto him to continue forty and two months."
✝   Revelation 17:8-14, "[8]The beast that thou sawest was, and is not;
    and shall ascend out of the bottomless pit, and go into perdition: and
    they that dwell on the earth shall wonder, whose names were not
    written in the book of life from the foundation of the world, when they
    behold the beast that was, and is not, and yet is. [9]And here is the mind
    which hath wisdom. The seven heads are seven mountains, on which
    the woman sitteth. [10]And there are seven kings: five are fallen, and
    one is, and the other is not yet come; and when he cometh, he must
    continue a short space. [11]And the beast that was, and is not, even he
    is the eighth, and is of the seven, and goeth into perdition. [12]And the
    ten horns which thou sawest are ten kings, which have received no
    kingdom as yet; but receive power as kings one hour with the beast.
    [13]These have one mind, and shall give their power and strength unto
    the beast. [14]These shall make war with the Lamb, and the Lamb shall

*overcome them: for he is Lord of lords, and King of kings: and they
that are with him are called, and chosen, and faithful."*

The little horn that Daniel sees in chapter 7 is the same little horn in
Revelation 13. The little horn is the Antichrist. He will rise to power
from one of the ten future kings. He will have seven horns, ten heads
and ten crowns. He will look like a leopard; have feet like a bear, and a
mouth like the mouth of a lion. Notice the beasts in Revelation 13 are
the reverse order of Daniel 7 (lion, bear, leopard). Recall that Daniel
prophesied from the beginning of the Age of the Gentiles therefore,
he is speaking of Babylon. Apostle John's viewpoint stands at the end
of the Age of the Gentiles.

✝ Daniel 7:21, *"I beheld, and the same horn made war with the saints,
and prevailed against them;"*

✝ Revelation 13:1-2, *"¹And I stood upon the sand of the sea, and saw
a beast rise up out of the sea, having seven heads and ten horns,
and upon his horns ten crowns, and upon his heads the name of
blasphemy. ²And the beast which I saw was like unto a leopard, and
his feet were as the feet of a bear, and his mouth as the mouth of a
lion: and the dragon gave him his power, and his seat, and great
authority."*

The Antichrist will have no regard for God or for the desire of women.
There is much discussion on what this verse actually means. It may
mean that he does not have the desire to marry or have conjugal
affection or relationship. Daniel 11:37 may have some agreement with
1 Timothy 4:1-5.

✝ Daniel 11:37, *"Neither shall he regard the God of his fathers, nor the
desire of women, nor regard any god: for he shall magnify himself
above all."*

✝ First Timothy 4:1-5, *"¹Now the Spirit speaketh expressly, that in the
latter times some shall depart from the faith, giving heed to seducing
spirits, and doctrines of devils; ²Speaking lies in hypocrisy; having*

their conscience seared with a hot iron; ³Forbidding to marry, and commanding to abstain from meats, which God hath created to be received with thanksgiving of them which believe and know the truth. ⁴For every creature of God is good, and nothing to be refused, if it be received with thanksgiving: ⁵For it is sanctified by the word of God and prayer."

FALSE PROPHET

Have you noticed the word fake in the news lately? Seems like the world is preparing for fake! The False Prophet acts like the Holy Spirit but is a phony. He will have supernatural power and will perform counterfeit miracles as he tries to impersonate the Holy Spirit. The False Prophet will coerce each person to take the mark of the beast (Revelation 13:16-17).

✝ Second Thessalonians 2:9, *"Even him, whose coming is after the working of Satan with all power and signs and lying wonders,"*

✝ Revelation 13:12-14, *"¹²And he exerciseth all the power of the first beast before him, and causeth the earth and them which dwell therein to worship the first beast, whose deadly wound was healed. ¹³And he doeth great wonders, so that he maketh fire come down from heaven on the earth in the sight of men, ¹⁴And deceiveth them that dwell on the earth by the means of those miracles which he had power to do in the sight of the beast; saying to them that dwell on the earth, that they should make an image to the beast, which had the wound by a sword, and did live."*

✝ Revelation 13:16-17, *"¹⁶And he causeth all, both small and great, rich and poor, free and bond, to receive a mark in their right hand, or in their foreheads: ¹⁷And that no man might buy or sell, save he that had the mark, or the name of the beast, or the number of his name ¹⁸ Here is wisdom. Let him that hath understanding count the number of the beast: for it is the number of a man; and his number is Six hundred threescore and six."*

† Revelation 19:20, *"And the beast was taken, and with him the false prophet that wrought miracles before him, with which he deceived them that had received the mark of the beast, and them that worshipped his image. These both were cast alive into a lake of fire burning with brimstone."*

The Bible warns us to beware of false prophets.

† Matthew 7:15, *¹⁵Beware of false prophets, which come to you in sheep's clothing, but inwardly they are ravening wolves."*

The False Prophet is the second beast seen in Revelation 13:11-18. He speaks like a dragon and has horns like a lamb. Horns represent strength and power while a lamb represents gentleness, but the false prophet will be an imitation of gentleness. He will exercise great power with deceptive gentleness, luring, performing miracles and coercing people. He will come out of the earth rather than the sea like the Antichrist. The False Prophet coerces everyone to take the Mark of the Beast.

† Revelation 13:11, *"And I beheld another beast coming up out of the earth; and he had two horns like a lamb, and he spake as a dragon.* He and the Antichrist will be thrown into the Lake of Fire.

† Revelation 19:20, *"And the beast was taken, and with him the false prophet that wrought miracles before him, with which he deceived them that had received the mark of the beast, and them that worshipped his image. These both were cast alive into a lake of fire burning with brimstone."*

† Revelation 20:7-10 shows that Satan will not be cast in the lake of fire at this time but will be later after the Millennium. This passage confirms the Beast and False Prophet will already be there.

† Revelation 20:7-10, *"⁷And when the thousand years are expired, Satan shall be loosed out of his prison, ⁸And shall go out to deceive the nations which are in the four quarters of the earth, Gog and Magog, to gather them together to battle: the number of whom is as*

the sand of the sea. ⁹And they went up on the breadth of the earth, and compassed the camp of the saints about, and the beloved city: and fire came down from God out of heaven, and devoured them. ¹⁰And the devil that deceived them was cast into the lake of fire and brimstone, where the beast and the false prophet are, and shall be tormented day and night for ever and ever."

The unholy trinity will be given all of the authority to reign. During the Tribulation, God is on His throne in Heaven and Jesus is with the saints in Heaven. Currently the Holy Spirit holds Satan back but a time will come during the Tribulation when he will be taken out of the way or removed so the unholy trinity will perform his work.

† Second Thessalonians: 2:7-8, *"⁷For the mystery of iniquity doth already work: only he who now letteth will let, until he be taken out of the way. ⁸And then shall that Wicked be revealed, whom the Lord shall consume with the spirit of his mouth, and shall destroy with the brightness of his coming:"*

† Revelation 7:15, *"Therefore are they before the throne of God, and serve him day and night in his temple: and he that sitteth on the throne shall dwell among them."*

† First Thessalonians 4:17, *"Then we which are alive and remain shall be caught up together with them in the clouds, to meet the Lord in the air: and so shall we ever be with the Lord."*

† Revelation 4: 4-11, *"⁴And round about the throne were four and twenty seats: and upon the seats I saw four and twenty elders sitting, clothed in white raiment; and they had on their heads crowns of gold. ⁵And out of the throne proceeded lightnings and thunderings and voices: and there were seven lamps of fire burning before the throne, which are the seven Spirits of God. ⁶And before the throne there was a sea of glass like unto crystal: and in the midst of the throne, and round about the throne, were four beasts full of eyes before and behind. ⁷And the first beast was like a lion, and the second beast like a calf, and the third beast had a face as a man, and the fourth beast was like a flying eagle. ⁸And the four beasts had each*

of them six wings about him; and they were full of eyes within: and they rest not day and night, saying, Holy, holy, holy, Lord God Almighty, which was, and is, and is to come. ⁹And when those beasts give glory and honour and thanks to him that sat on the throne, who liveth for ever and ever, ¹⁰The four and twenty elders fall down before him that sat on the throne, and worship him that liveth for ever and ever, and cast their crowns before the throne, saying, ¹¹Thou art worthy, O Lord, to receive glory and honour and power: for thou hast created all things, and for thy pleasure they are and were created."

The meaning of "taken out of the way" has caused some discussion among many. Since the Holy Spirit has been taken out of the way who can save the people during the Tribulation?" This phrase means the enemy will no longer be held back and will be allowed to rule using his most harsh and evil methods. This refers to the fact that the Holy Spirit will not restrain Satan or hold him back. I don't believe this means that the Holy Spirit will not be available to work in those who want to be saved. The Bible doesn't teach that the Holy Spirit is not at work still but rather is allowing Satan to do whatever he wills without any restraining influence. People will still get saved during the Tribulation and will be called Tribulation Saints. The question on how can they be convicted without the Holy Spirit is still pondered. Yes, God is everywhere at the same time (omnipresent) but during this time of Tribulation Satan is ruling and the Holy Sprit is no longer confining him so how can they be saved without the conviction of the Holy Spirit? One explanation could be they are saved much like those in the Old Testament and pre-Pentecost. One teaching claims the Holy Spirit will be present during the Tribulation yet the Bible clearly teaches the Holy Spirit will be taken out of the way (Second Thessalonian 2:7-8). The two witnesses and the 144,000 Jews will communicate the message of salvation and hope during the Tribulation so the Holy Spirit must still be at work. Revelation 7:9 infers a great multitude will be saved that no man can number. Whatever way God chooses to save many during the Tribulation may be a point of opinion for us, but the Bible clearly teaches there will be Tribulation Saints.

Zechariah 13:7-8 teaches that one-third of the Jews will survive the Tribulation.

† Zechariah 13:7-8, *"⁷Awake, O sword, against my shepherd, and against the man that is my fellow, saith the L*ORD *of hosts: smite the shepherd, and the sheep shall be scattered: and I will turn mine hand upon the little ones. ⁸And it shall come to pass, that in all the land, saith the L*ORD*, two parts therein shall be cut off and die; but the third shall be left therein."*

† Second Thessalonians 2:7-8, *"⁷For the mystery of iniquity doth already work: only he who now letteth will let, until he be taken out of the way. ⁸And then shall that Wicked be revealed, whom the Lord shall consume with the spirit of his mouth, and shall destroy with the brightness of his coming:"*

† Revelation 3:4, *"Thou hast a few names even in Sardis which have not defiled their garments; and they shall walk with me in white: for they are worthy."*

† Revelation 6:9-11, *"⁹And when he had opened the fifth seal, I saw under the altar the souls of them that were slain for the word of God, and for the testimony which they held: ¹⁰And they cried with a loud voice, saying, How long, O Lord, holy and true, dost thou not judge and avenge our blood on them that dwell on the earth? ¹¹And white robes were given unto every one of them; and it was said unto them, that they should rest yet for a little season, until their fellow servants also and their brethren, that should be killed as they were, should be fulfilled."*

† Revelation 7:9-14, *"⁹After this I beheld, and, lo, a great multitude, which no man could number, of all nations, and kindreds, and people, and tongues, stood before the throne, and before the Lamb, clothed with white robes, and palms in their hands; ¹⁰And cried with a loud voice, saying, Salvation to our God which sitteth upon the throne, and unto the Lamb. ¹¹And all the angels stood round about the throne, and about the elders and the four beasts, and fell before the throne on their faces, and worshipped God, ¹²Saying, Amen: Blessing, and glory, and wisdom, and thanksgiving, and honour, and power, and might, be unto our God for ever and ever. Amen. ¹³And one of the*

elders answered, saying unto me, What are these which are arrayed in white robes? and whence came they?[14] And I said unto him, Sir, thou knowest. And he said to me, These are they which came out of great tribulation, and have washed their robes, and made them white in the blood of the Lamb."

✝ Revelation 11:3-12, *"[3]And I will give power unto my two witnesses, and they shall prophesy a thousand two hundred and threescore days, clothed in sackcloth. [4]These are the two olive trees, and the two candlesticks standing before the God of the earth. [5]And if any man will hurt them, fire proceedeth out of their mouth, and devoureth their enemies: and if any man will hurt them, he must in this manner be killed. [6]These have power to shut heaven, that it rain not in the days of their prophecy: and have power over waters to turn them to blood, and to smite the earth with all plagues, as often as they will. [7]And when they shall have finished their testimony, the beast that ascendeth out of the bottomless pit shall make war against them, and shall overcome them, and kill them. [8]And their dead bodies shall lie in the street of the great city, which spiritually is called Sodom and Egypt, where also our Lord was crucified. [9]And they of the people and kindreds and tongues and nations shall see their dead bodies three days and an half, and shall not suffer their dead bodies to be put in graves. [10]And they that dwell upon the earth shall rejoice over them, and make merry, and shall send gifts one to another; because these two prophets tormented them that dwelt on the earth. [11]And after three days and an half the spirit of life from God entered into them, and they stood upon their feet; and great fear fell upon them which saw them. [12]And they heard a great voice from heaven saying unto them, Come up hither. And they ascended up to heaven in a cloud; and their enemies beheld them."*

✝ Revelation 20:4, *"And I saw thrones, and they sat upon them, and judgment was given unto them: and I saw the souls of them that were beheaded for the witness of Jesus, and for the word of God, and which had not worshipped the beast, neither his image, neither had received his mark upon their foreheads, or in their hands; and they lived and reigned with Christ a thousand years."*

HOLY TRINITY AND UNHOLY
SATANIC TRINITY COMPARED

Holy Trinity	Scripture For Holy Trinity	Unholy Satanic Trinity	Scripture for Unholy Trinity
God is The Father	1st Corinthians 8:6 6 But to us there is but one God, the Father, of whom are all things, and we in him; and one Lord Jesus Christ, by whom are all things, and we by him. Matthew 28:19 19 Go ye therefore, and teach all nations, baptizing them in the name of the Father, and of the Son, and of the Holy Ghost:	The Dragon is The Anti-God	Revelation 12:9 9And the great dragon was cast out, that old serpent, called the Devil, and Satan, which deceiveth the whole world: he was cast out into the earth, and his angels were cast out with him. Revelation 20:2 2 And he laid hold on the dragon, that old serpent, which is the Devil, and Satan, and bound him a thousand years,
God the Son is Jesus Christ	John 1:14 14 And the Word was made flesh, and dwelt among us, (and we beheld his glory, the glory as of the only begotten of the Father,) full of grace and truth. John 10:30 I and my Father are one. John 12:45 And he that seeth me seeth him that sent me.	The Beast The Son of Perdition is The Anti-Christ	2 Thessalonians 2:3 3 Let no man deceive you by any means: for that day shall not come, except there come a falling away first, and that man of sin be revealed, the son of perdition; Revelation 13: 4-5 4And they worshipped the dragon which gave power unto the beast: and they worshipped the beast, saying, Who is like unto the beast? who is able to make war with him? 5And there was given unto him a mouth speaking great things and blasphemies; and power was given unto him to continue forty and two months.
God the Spirit is The Holy Spirit	2nd Corinthians 3:17 17Now the Lord is that Spirit: and where the Spirit of the Lord is, there is liberty. Matthew 3:16 16And Jesus, when he was baptized, went up straightway out of the water: and, lo, the heavens were opened unto him, and he saw the Spirit of God descending like a dove, and lighting upon him:	The False Prophet is The Anti-Spirit	Revelation 19:20 And the beast was taken, and with him the false prophet that wrought miracles before him, with which he deceived them that had received the mark of the beast, and them that worshipped his image. These both were cast alive into a lake of fire burning with brimstone. Revelation 20:10 And the devil that deceived them was cast into the lake of fire and brimstone, where the beast and the false prophet are, and shall be tormented day and night for ever and ever.

RECOMMENDED ACTIVITIES

1. Study Antiochus Epiphanes from history. He is considered an Antichrist prototype. Which of his characteristics resemble the Antichrist?
2. Use your Strong's concordance and find the only two books where the word Antichrist/s is used five times. It is found in four verses and twice in one verse. Hint: First John and Second John.
3. Study the scriptures given in chapter ten of this book (Unholy Trinity) in other translations, such as English Standard Version, or New American Standard Bible.
4. Study Daniel 11:37 in various reputable commentaries and resources.

PERSONAL NOTES

CHAPTER ELEVEN

THE BATTLE OF ARMAGEDDON

The word Armageddon ("Har-Megedon") appears only once in the Bible: Revelation 16:16, "And he gathered them together into a place called in the Hebrew tongue Armageddon." It will be the deadliest and the bloodiest battle in world history and will be fought toward the end of the Tribulation. Troops will gather at Mount Megiddo. In fact, the word Armageddon means hill or city of Megiddo.

At the beginning of the Tribulation Satan will begin to establish his throne and kingdom as a one-world government, one-world religion, and a New World Order. The spirit of the Antichrist is already at work. We can see the efforts in our day to make a one-world government, for example, the open borders debate, World Bank, World Health Organization, the European Union, World Trade Organization, and the United Nations. No one will know that the Antichrist is the world ruler because he is bringing a false peace out of the chaos after the Rapture. He will attempt to mimic Christ, the true Incarnate, but rather he is a Satan incarnate, Revelation 13. However, at the Middle of the Tribulation he will be revealed as the Antichrist and will dominate as the world ruler. At the beginning he has few challenges to his rule and powers but during the Tribulation the various judgments of seals, trumpets, and vials highlight that he is a fake! Yet, Satan will think he can still win and dominate the world forever. He will cause the world to worship the Antichrist and take the mark of the beast on either their right hand or on their forehead.

> ✝ Revelation 13:16, *"And he causeth all, both small and great, rich and poor, free and bond, to receive a mark in their right hand, or in their foreheads:"*

He will still believe that he is God and that he will be forever. But God will return with His saints and Holy angels at the Battle of Armageddon toward the end of the Tribulation, which will mark the beginning of the Second Coming of Jesus Christ. He will come as a fierce warrior, like a lion instead of a lamb, to demonstrate His complete and awesome power and wrath over the enemy and upon those who rejected Him.

> ✝ Revelation 16:13-21, *"[13]And I saw three unclean spirits like frogs come out of the mouth of the dragon, and out of the mouth of the beast, and out of the mouth of the false prophet. [14]For they are the spirits of devils, working miracles, which go forth unto the kings of the earth and of the whole world, to gather them to the battle of that great day of God Almighty. [15]Behold, I come as a thief. Blessed is he that watcheth, and keepeth his garments, lest he walk naked, and they see his shame. [16]And he gathered them together into a place called in the Hebrew tongue Armageddon. [17]And the seventh angel poured out his vial into the air; and there came a great voice out of the temple of heaven, from the throne, saying, It is done. [18]And there were voices, and thunders, and lightnings; and there was a great earthquake, such as was not since men were upon the earth, so mighty an earthquake, and so great. [19]And the great city was divided into three parts, and the cities of the nations fell: and great Babylon came in remembrance before God, to give unto her the cup of the wine of the fierceness of*

his wrath. [20]And every island fled away, and the mountains were not found. [21]And there fell upon men a great hail out of heaven, every stone about the weight of a talent: and men blasphemed God because of the plague of the hail; for the plague thereof was exceeding great."

Zechariah told of this battle in Zechariah 14:1-3.

†   Zechariah 14:1-3, *"[1]Behold, the day of the LORD cometh, and thy spoil shall be divided in the midst of thee. [2]For I will gather all nations against Jerusalem to battle; and the city shall be taken, and the houses rifled, and the women ravished; and half of the city shall go forth into captivity, and the residue of the people shall not be cut off from the city. [3]Then shall the LORD go forth, and fight against those nations, as when he fought in the day of battle."*

The events of the Battle of Armageddon end the Tribulation. The armies of the Antichrist will be destroyed. The Antichrist and False Prophet will be captured and cast into the Lake of Fire. All nations of the world will be called to gather at Mount Megiddo. The entire world will be involved. The blood of this battle will run for a thousand and six hundred furlongs or two hundred miles and will be up to the horses' bridles. This battle concludes the Tribulation and begins the Second Coming of Jesus. He will come on a white horse, eyes with flames of fire, and He will wear many crowns on His head as the Victor! He will come <u>with</u> His saints unlike at the Rapture where He will come <u>for</u> the saints.

†   Revelation 14:14-20, *"[14]And I looked, and behold a white cloud, and upon the cloud one sat like unto the Son of man, having on his head a golden crown, and in his hand a sharp sickle. [15]And another angel came out of the temple, crying with a loud voice to him that sat on the cloud, Thrust in thy sickle, and reap: for the time is come for thee to reap; for the harvest of the earth is ripe. [16]And he that sat on the cloud thrust in his sickle on the earth; and the earth was reaped. [17]And another angel came out of the temple which is in heaven, he also having a sharp sickle.* [18]*And another angel came out from the altar, which had power over fire; and cried with a loud cry to him that had the sharp sickle, saying, Thrust in thy sharp sickle, and gather the clusters of the vine of the earth; for her grapes are fully ripe.* [19]*And the angel thrust in his sickle into the earth, and gathered the vine of the earth, and cast it into the great winepress of the wrath of God.* [20]*And the winepress was trodden without the city, and blood came out of the winepress, even unto the horse bridles, by the space of a thousand and six hundred furlongs."*

✝ Isaiah 34:1-8, *"*[1]*Come near, ye nations, to hear; and hearken, ye people: let the earth hear, and all that is therein; the world, and all things that come forth of it.* [2] *For the indignation of the LORD is upon all nations, and his fury upon all their armies: he hath utterly destroyed them, he hath delivered them to the slaughter.* [3] *Their slain also shall be cast out, and their stink shall come up out of their carcases, and the mountains shall be melted with their blood.* [4]*And all the host of heaven shall be dissolved, and the heavens shall be rolled together as a scroll: and all their host shall fall down, as the leaf falleth off from the vine, and as a falling fig from the fig tree.* [5]*For my sword shall be bathed in heaven: behold, it shall come down upon Idumea, and upon the people of my curse, to judgment.* [6]*The sword of the LORD is filled with blood, it is made fat with fatness, and with the blood of lambs and goats, with the fat of the kidneys of rams: for the LORD hath a sacrifice in Bozrah, and a great slaughter in the land of Idumea.* [7]*And the unicorns shall come down with them, and the bullocks with the bulls; and their land shall be soaked with blood, and their dust made fat with fatness.* [8]*For it is the day of the LORD's vengeance, and the year of recompences for the controversy of Zion."*

✝ Revelation 19:11-16, *"*[11]*And I saw heaven opened, and behold a white horse; and he that sat upon him was called Faithful and True, and in righteousness he doth judge and make war.* [12]*His eyes were as a flame of fire, and on his head were many crowns; and he had a name written, that no man knew, but he himself.* [13]*And he was clothed with a vesture dipped in blood: and his name is called The Word of God.* [14]*And the armies which were in heaven followed him upon white* *horses, clothed in fine linen, white and clean. ^{15}And out of his mouth goeth a sharp sword, that with it he should smite the nations: and he shall rule them with a rod of iron: and he treadeth the winepress of the fierceness and wrath of Almighty God. ^{16}And he hath on his vesture and on his thigh a name written, KING OF KINGS, AND LORD OF LORDS."*

The saints will not have to fight in this battle. The saints of God will only watch what happens in the battle. Jesus is the only one with a weapon. Out of His mouth will be a sharp sword, which is the Word of God. At creation (Genesis 1) He spoke the world into existence. In Genesis 17, God spoke to Abram and he fell on his face. When Jesus was arrested at the Garden of Gethsemane, He spoke the words, "I am he" and the soldiers fell to the ground. When God speaks at the Battle of Armageddon, evil will be destroyed! Revelation 19:13 expresses that His clothes will be dipped in blood but the saints still have clean white linens and that He Himself will rule with the rod.

† John 18:4-6, *"^{4}Jesus therefore, knowing all things that should come upon him, went forth, and said unto them, Whom seek ye? ^{5}They answered him, Jesus of Nazareth. Jesus saith unto them, I am he. And Judas also, which betrayed him, stood with them. ^{6}As soon then as he had said unto them, I am he, they went backward, and fell to the ground".*

† Revelation 19:13, *"And he was clothed with a vesture dipped in blood: and his name is called The Word of God."*

The Battle of Armageddon will end when all are dead, Antichrist and False Prophet are captured and thrown into the Lake of Fire, when Satan is captured and bound for one thousand years, and with a feast called the Supper of the Great God. Revelation 19 reveals the end of the Battle of Armageddon marked by the capturing of the Antichrist and the False Prophet. The capture of Satan is discussed in Revelation 20. Satan will be captured and bound for one thousand years. His doom will come at the end of the Millennium.

† Revelation 20:1-3, *"¹And I saw an angel come down from heaven, having the key of the bottomless pit and a great chain in his hand. ²And he laid hold on the dragon, that old serpent, which is the Devil, and Satan, and bound him a thousand years, ³And cast him into the bottomless pit, and shut him up, and set a seal upon him, that he should deceive the nations no more, till the thousand years should be fulfilled: and after that he must be loosed a little season."*

The supper of the great God is described in Ezekiel 39 and Revelation 19. It marks the end of the Battle of Armageddon with a feast for the birds called the Supper of the Great God. Do not confuse it with the Marriage Supper of the Lamb!

† Ezekiel 39:17- 20, *"¹⁷And, thou son of man, thus saith the Lord GOD; Speak unto every feathered fowl, and to every beast of the field, Assemble yourselves, and come; gather yourselves on every side to my sacrifice that I do sacrifice for you, even a great sacrifice upon the mountains of Israel, that ye may eat flesh, and drink blood. ¹⁸Ye shall eat the flesh of the mighty, and drink the blood of the princes of the earth, of rams, of lambs, and of goats, of bullocks, all of them fatlings of Bashan. ¹⁹And ye shall eat fat till ye be full, and drink blood till ye be drunken, of my sacrifice which I have sacrificed for you. ²⁰Thus ye shall be filled at my table with horses and chariots, with mighty men, and with all men of war, saith the Lord GOD."*

† Matthew 24:27-28, *"²⁷For as the lightning cometh out of the east, and shineth even unto the west; so shall also the coming of the Son of man be. ²⁸For wheresoever the carcase is, there will the eagles be gathered together."*

† Revelation 19:17, *"And I saw an angel standing in the sun; and he cried with a loud voice, saying to all the fowls that fly in the midst of heaven, Come and gather yourselves together unto the supper of the great God;"*

† Revelation 19:19-21, *"¹⁹And I saw the beast, and the kings of the earth, and their armies, gathered together to make war against him that sat on the horse, and against his army. ²⁰And the beast was*

taken, and with him the false prophet that wrought miracles before him, with which he deceived them that had received the mark of the beast, and them that worshipped his image. These both were cast alive into a lake of fire burning with brimstone. [21] And the remnant were slain with the sword of him that sat upon the horse, which sword proceeded out of his mouth: and all the fowls were filled with their flesh."

RECOMMENDED ACTIVITIES

1. Study where the Mount Megiddo is located. Learn about its history.
2. Study Revelation chapters 19 and 20. Read it in various versions.
3. Study more on the Supper of the Great God. Commentaries will be useful.
4. It is good to read other authors' materials to compare notes of various authors and to clarify and confirm information. Be absolutely sure it is a reputable source. Many authors come from different viewpoints. Others are out and out false prophets. So study the faith beliefs of your authors. Read and study any Tribulation or the end times material written by Dr. David Jeremiah. His website offers reliable and scholarly resources. https://www.davidjeremiah.org/. Another author who is highly knowledgeable in this area is Dr. John Hagee. His website and books will be helpful also for more advanced studies as well. https://www.jhm.org.

CHAPTER TWELVE

THE SECOND COMING

The Second Coming of Jesus is the return of Jesus to earth after His initial birth, death, resurrection and ascension. His purpose will be to overthrow Satan, the Antichrist, and the False Prophet and to establish His kingdom on earth. He will abolish evil, the Antichrist, and the False Prophet and He will establish His millennial kingdom. The Second Coming of Jesus Christ occurs at the end of the Tribulation during the Battle of Armageddon as was discussed in the last chapter. The New Testament saints of God taken up during the Rapture will sit before the Judgment Seat and receive their glorified bodies. There will be a wedding in heaven. It will be the Marriage of the Lamb to His Bride prior to the Second Coming. The Marriage Supper of the Lamb will come later.

† Revelation 19:7-8, *"⁷Let us be glad and rejoice, and give honour to him: for the marriage of the Lamb is come, and his wife hath made herself ready. ⁸And to her was granted that she should be arrayed in fine linen, clean and white: for the fine linen is the righteousness of saints."*

As discussed earlier, Old Testament saints and Tribulation saints will be resurrected before the end of the Tribulation. While Jesus came for the saints during the Rapture, He will come with the saints and angels at the Second Coming during the Battle of Armageddon. The saints and the angels are the armies of God but we will not fight in the battle.

† Zechariah 14:5, *"And ye shall flee to the valley of the mountains; for the valley of the mountains shall reach unto Azal: yea, ye shall flee, like as ye fled from before the earthquake in the days of Uzziah king of Judah: and the* Lord *my God shall come, and all the saints with thee."*

† Matthew 16:27, *"For the Son of man shall come in the glory of his Father with his angels; and then he shall reward every man according to his works."*

† Matthew 25:31, *"When the Son of man shall come in his glory, and all the holy angels with him, then shall he sit upon the throne of his glory:'*

† Luke 9:26, *"For whosoever shall be ashamed of me and of my words, of him shall the Son of man be ashamed, when he shall come in his own glory, and in his Father's, and of the holy angels."*

† Mark 8:38, *"Whosoever therefore shall be ashamed of me and of my words in this adulterous and sinful generation; of him also shall the Son of man be ashamed, when he cometh in the glory of his Father with the holy angels."*

† Luke 12:8, *"Also I say unto you, Whosoever shall confess me before men, him shall the Son of man also confess before the angels of God:"*

† First Thessalonians 3:13, *"To the end he may stablish your hearts unblameable in holiness before God, even our Father, at the coming of our Lord Jesus Christ with all his saints."*

† Jude 1:14, *"And Enoch also, the seventh from Adam, prophesied of these, saying, Behold, the Lord cometh with ten thousands of his saints,"*

† Revelation 19:14, *"And the armies which were in heaven followed him upon white horses, clothed in fine linen, white and clean."*

Believing survivors of the Tribulation will not be resurrected and will go into the Millennium with mortal bodies.

† Matthew 24:13, *"But he that shall endure unto the end, the same shall be saved."*

At the Second Coming when Jesus comes to execute judgment on non-believers, He will not be quiet and humble as He did at the First Coming. They will see Him coming in the clouds (Revelation 1:7). He will be a warrior riding on His white horse (Revelation 19:11). It will not be like a thief in the night as was the Rapture. The time of His coming is not known but the coming will be visible for all to see and hear. Matthew 24:27 describes it like lightening coming out of the east. He will come as the King in power, authority, glory, and honor and the entire world will know that He and He alone is God. All nations will mourn. He will come in the east upon the Mount of Olives and the mountain will split (Zechariah 14:4). The Antichrist will already be gathered with his armies in the "valley of Jehoshaphat" (Joel 3: 2, 12).

† Joel 3:2, *"I will also gather all nations, and will bring them down into the valley of Jehoshaphat, and will plead with them there for my people and for my heritage Israel, whom they have scattered among the nations, and parted my land"*

† Joel 3:12, *"Let the heathen be wakened, and come up to the valley of Jehoshaphat: for there will I sit to judge all the heathen round about."*

† Zechariah 14:4, *"And his feet shall stand in that day upon the mount of Olives, which is before Jerusalem on the east, and the mount of Olives shall cleave in the midst thereof toward the east and toward the west, and there shall be a very great valley; and half of the mountain shall remove toward the north, and half of it toward the south."*

† Matthew 24:27, *"For as the lightning cometh out of the east, and shineth even unto the west; so shall also the coming of the Son of man be."*

† Matthew 24:30, *"And then shall appear the sign of the Son of man in heaven: and then shall all the tribes of the earth mourn, and they shall see the Son of man coming in the clouds of heaven with power and great glory."*

✝ Matthew 25: 30-32, *"³⁰And cast ye the unprofitable servant into outer darkness: there shall be weeping and gnashing of teeth. ³¹When the Son of man shall come in his glory, and all the holy angels with him, then shall he sit upon the throne of his glory: ³²And before him shall be gathered all nations: and he shall separate them one from another, as a shepherd divideth his sheep from the goats:"*

✝ Acts 1:11, *"Which also said, Ye men of Galilee, why stand ye gazing up into heaven? this same Jesus, which is taken up from you into heaven, shall so come in like manner as ye have seen him go into heaven."*

✝ Revelation 1:7, *"Behold, he cometh with clouds; and every eye shall see him, and they also which pierced him: and all kindreds of the earth shall wail because of him. Even so, Amen."*

✝ Revelation 19:11, *"And I saw heaven opened, and behold a white horse; and he that sat upon him was called Faithful and True, and in righteousness he doth judge and make war."*

PERSONAL NOTES

CHAPTER THIRTEEN

THE MARRIAGE SUPPER OF THE LAMB

The Marriage of the Lamb and the Marriage Supper of the Lamb are related but two separate events. A marriage in Biblical days was different than a western wedding known today. The marriage consisted of at least three phases. The first phase was the agreement and contract signing between the parents. It is also called the "ketubbah", covenant, betrothal or the legal phase. During this phase a dowry is paid for the bride. This phase represents the time of our conversion. Betrothal is a picture of salvation. Jesus paid our dowry with His life and blood on the cross of Calvary. This was the phase Mary and Joseph were in when the Holy Spirit made filled her womb with Jesus. We are living in the betrothal period waiting to be united with our Bridegroom. A New Testament saint, who is the Church, is the bride to be. However, Jesus had to ascend to heaven. He had to go prepare a place for His bride.

✝ John 14:3, *"And if I go and prepare a place for you, I will come again, and receive you unto myself; that where I am, there ye may be also."*

The second phase is when the bridegroom returned for his bride. The bridegroom had up to seven years to collect the money and prepare a place for his bride. He would notify the father of the bride when all conditions of the contract were met and they would set a date for consummation. The bride was made aware that he would be coming at midnight in a torch lit parade. She would be ready and waiting for the bridegroom. This second phase is called "chuppah" or sexual consummation. The parable of the ten virgins illustrates this phase best in Matthew 25:1-3. The church waits for the time when the Bridegroom returns for His bride, the church. Sometime after the Rapture and the Judgment Seat the church will unite with the Bridegroom. This Marriage of the Lamb event will occur in Heaven. Just so that you are aware, some dispute that the church is the Bride and argue that Israel is the Bride of Christ.

The third phase is that of a feast called the Marriage Supper of the Lamb. After consummation the entire wedding party would have a procession to the house of the bridegroom for the wedding feast, which represents the Marriage Supper of the Lamb. It is illustrated in John 2 after the marriage took place and lasted for days or even weeks. It is a great celebration with songs of Alleluia before the Lord.

Revelation 19:6-10 speaks to a Marriage Supper of the Lamb.

† Revelation 19:6-10, *"⁶And I heard as it were the voice of a great multitude, and as the voice of many waters, and as the voice of mighty thunderings, saying, Alleluia: for the Lord God omnipotent reigneth. ⁷Let us be glad and rejoice, and give honour to him: for the marriage of the Lamb is come, and his wife hath made herself ready. ⁸And to her was granted that she should be arrayed in fine linen, clean and white: for the fine linen is the righteousness of saints. ⁹And he saith unto me, Write, Blessed are they which are called unto the marriage supper of the Lamb. And he saith unto me, These are the true sayings of God. ¹⁰And I fell at his feet to worship him. And he said unto me, See thou do it not: I am thy fellow servant, and of thy brethren that*

have the testimony of Jesus: worship God: for the testimony of Jesus
is the spirit of prophecy."

There are two views on where the wedding supper takes place. The first view is that the marriage supper will take place in heaven after the Rapture and before the Tribulation ends.

The second view is the marriage supper will take place on earth. Jesus is the Bridegroom and the center of attraction. The Church is the Bride of Christ. There are other invited guests at the supper: Israel, who is saved during the Tribulation, the resurrected Old Testament saints and those Tribulation saints who survive the Tribulation. The Israel converts and the survivors of the Tribulation will not be resurrected but will remain on earth and will go into the Millennium with their mortal bodies. They will not have glorified bodies. Therefore, the marriage supper is thought to take place on earth. The scriptures below infer suppertime on earth.

† Matthew 22:1-14, "¹And Jesus answered and spake unto them again by parables, and said, ²*The kingdom of heaven is like unto a certain king, which made a marriage for his son,* ³*And sent forth his servants to call them that were bidden to the wedding: and they would not come.* ⁴*Again, he sent forth other servants, saying, Tell them, which are bidden, Behold, I have prepared my dinner: my oxen and my fatlings are killed, and all things are ready: come unto the marriage.* ⁵*But they made light of it, and went their ways, one to his farm, another to his merchandise:* ⁶*And the remnant took his servants, and entreated them spitefully, and slew them.* ⁷*But when the king heard thereof, he was wroth: and he sent forth his armies, and destroyed those murderers, and burned up their city.* ⁸*Then saith he to his servants, The wedding is ready, but they which were bidden were not worthy.* ⁹*Go ye therefore into the highways, and as many as ye shall find, bid to the marriage.* ¹⁰*So those servants went out into the highways, and gathered together all as many as they found, both bad and good: and the wedding was furnished with guests.* ¹¹*And*

when the king came in to see the guests, he saw there a man which had not on a wedding garment: ¹²And he saith unto him, Friend, how camest thou in hither not having a wedding garment? And he was speechless. ¹³Then said the king to the servants, Bind him hand and foot, and take him away, and cast him into outer darkness, there shall be weeping and gnashing of teeth. ¹⁴For many are called, but few are chosen."

† Matthew 25:1-13, "¹Then shall the kingdom of heaven be likened unto ten virgins, which took their lamps, and went forth to meet the bridegroom. ²And five of them were wise, and five were foolish. ³They that were foolish took their lamps, and took no oil with them: ⁴But the wise took oil in their vessels with their lamps. ⁵While the bridegroom tarried, they all slumbered and slept. ⁶And at midnight there was a cry made, Behold, the bridegroom cometh; go ye out to meet him. ⁷Then all those virgins arose, and trimmed their lamps. ⁸And the foolish said unto the wise, Give us of your oil; for our lamps are gone out. ⁹But the wise answered, saying, Not so; lest there be not enough for us and you: but go ye rather to them that sell, and buy for yourselves. ¹⁰And while they went to buy, the bridegroom came; and they that were ready went in with him to the marriage: and the door was shut. ¹¹Afterward came also the other virgins, saying, Lord, Lord, open to us. ¹²But he answered and said, Verily I say unto you, I know you not. ¹³Watch therefore, for ye know neither the day nor the hour wherein the Son of man cometh.

† Luke 14:16-25, "¹⁶Then said he unto him, A certain man made a great supper, and bade many: ¹⁷And sent his servant at supper time to say to them that were bidden, Come; for all things are now ready. ¹⁸And they all with one consent began to make excuse. The first said unto him, I have bought a piece of ground, and I must needs go and see it: I pray thee have me excused. ¹⁹And another said, I have bought five yoke of oxen, and I go to prove them: I pray thee have me excused. ²⁰And another said, I have married a wife, and therefore I cannot come. ²¹So that servant came, and shewed his lord these things. Then the master of the house being angry said to his servant, Go out quickly into the streets and lanes of the city, and bring in hither the poor, and

the maimed, and the halt, and the blind. [22]And the servant said, Lord, it is done as thou hast commanded, and yet there is room. [23]And the lord said unto the servant, Go out into the highways and hedges, and compel them to come in, that my house may be filled. [24]For I say unto you, That none of those men which were bidden shall taste of my supper. [25]And there went great multitudes with him: and he turned, and said unto them,"

✝ Revelation 19:7-9, "[7]Let us be glad and rejoice, and give honour to him: for the marriage of the Lamb is come, and his wife hath made herself ready. [8]And to her was granted that she should be arrayed in fine linen, clean and white: for the fine linen is the righteousness of saints. [9]And he saith unto me, Write, Blessed are they which are called unto the marriage supper of the Lamb. And he saith unto me, These are the true sayings of God."

PERSONAL NOTES

CHAPTER FOUTEEN

THE MILLENNIUM

The Millennium follows the events of Second Coming of Christ. The Millennium will be a thousand years reign of Christ on earth. Glorified saints will rule with Christ.

- ✝ First Corinthians 6:2, *"Do ye not know that the saints shall judge the world? and if the world shall be judged by you, are ye unworthy to judge the smallest matters?"*
- ✝ Second Timothy 2:12, *"If we suffer, we shall also reign with him: if we deny him, he also will deny us:"*
- ✝ Revelation 5:10, *"And hast made us unto our God kings and priests: and we shall reign on the earth."*
- ✝ Revelation 20:4, *"And I saw thrones, and they sat upon them, and judgment was given unto them: and I saw the souls of them that were beheaded for the witness of Jesus, and for the word of God, and which had not worshipped the beast, neither his image, neither had received his mark upon their foreheads, or in their hands; and they lived and reigned with Christ a thousand years."*

When will these 1000 years begin? No one knows except the Father. However, we can reflect upon one thoughtful consideration. Let's take the year 2020, for example.

Our Gregorian calendar says we are in year 2020 in the Year of our Lord. Prior to our Gregorian calendar, the Julian calendar was used but had many errors. A monk, mathematician, theologian, and scholar named Dionysius Exiguus developed a system that led to the descriptions of AD and BC and led to the more accurate Gregorian calendar that we use today. AD (*Anno Domini*) refers to after Christ or in the Year of our Lord and some use it to mean the beginning of the Christian era. BC refers to Before Christ. Exiguus' calculations were actually off somewhere between 4-6 years, dating the birth of Christ, however we still use the system he established. Jews do not believe in Jesus as Lord so they use a system of BCE and CE. BCE refers to Before the Common Era and CE refers to the Common Era.

While our calendar counts from the time of the birth of Christ, the Jewish calendar counts from about 3761 BCE. Maimonides, a Jewish philosopher, established this date that is said to be the date of Biblical creation. If we link the almost 4,000 years before Christ and approximately 2,000 years after Christ we find the total of about 6000 years. According to the Jewish year, we are currently in the year 5780 that is equivalent to our 2020 AD. To understand it more clearly, consider below:

5780 = current Jewish year (The Jewish New Year began in our 2019) Year 5781 will come in the middle of September 2020).

3761 = Biblical creation according to Hebrew thought (approximately 4000 years)

2020 = A. D. Gregorian calendar (approximately 2000 years)

3761 + 2020 = 5781 which is approximately 6000 years

4000 + 2000 = 6000 years or the end of the sixth millennium

These six thousand years are soon coming to a close. The seventh millennium (7000 years) is thought to correspond to the seventh day of the week or the day of rest.

Second Peter 3:8 says a day is as a thousand years, therefore let us consider that we are living in the sixth day. Hebrews 4:9 indicates there is a Sabbath rest still remaining--- See Strong's Number 4520 "sabbatismos". The Sabbath symbolizes the coming of Messiah who will provide a permanent rest for His people. Jesus is our Sabbath rest. No, I am not prophesying a day and hour or even a year of when the Rapture and Tribulation will occur. We are just looking at a thoughtful consideration that has been deliberated. We must not be carried away with predictions unless it is firmly set in the Word of God through the scriptures. While we do not know a time, day, year, or an hour, we can surmise that the Sabbath rest is near approaching. The absolute most important thing is that we are ready at all times and that we have given our life to Christ and repented of our sins.

† Second Peter 3:8, *"But, beloved, be not ignorant of this one thing, that one day is with the Lord as a thousand years, and a thousand years as one day."*

† Hebrews 4:9, *"There remaineth therefore a rest to the people of God."*

The term "a thousand years" is mentioned six times in Revelation 20: 2, 3, 4, 5, 6, and 7.

† Revelation 20, 2-7, *" ²And he laid hold on the dragon, that old serpent, which is the Devil, and Satan, and bound him a thousand years, ³And cast him into the bottomless pit, and shut him up, and set a seal upon him, that he should deceive the nations no more, till the thousand years should be fulfilled: and after that he must be loosed a little season. ⁴And I saw thrones, and they sat upon them, and judgment was given unto them: and I saw the souls of them that were beheaded for the witness of Jesus, and for the word of God, and which had not worshipped the beast, neither his image, neither had received his mark upon their foreheads, or in their hands; and they lived and reigned with Christ a thousand years. ⁵But the rest of the dead lived not again until the thousand years were finished. This is the first resurrection. ⁶Blessed and holy is he that hath part in the first resurrection: on such*

the second death hath no power, but they shall be priests of God and of Christ, and shall reign with him a thousand years. ⁷And when the thousand years are expired, Satan shall be loosed out of his prison,"

At the time of the Millennium, the Antichrist and the False Prophet will have already been cast into the lake of fire. Satan's time will not have come yet. He will be bound for a thousand years until the end when he will be loosed for a season. During the one thousand years, Satan will not be permitted to exercise his power and influence, nor will he have any impact on those in the Millennium until he is released for a little season.

> † Revelation 20:3, *"And cast him into the bottomless pit, and shut him up, and set a seal upon him, that he should deceive the nations no more, till the thousand years should be fulfilled: and after that he must be loosed a little season."*

All believers will populate the Millennium. Persons present at the Millennium will include:

1. Those believers raptured at the end of the Church Age as was discussed earlier.
2. Those believers who die before the Day of Pentecost, (the birth of the Church), along with those who die during the Tribulation as was previously discussed.
3. When Christ returns there will be saints on earth who survived the Battle of Armageddon. Those who survive The Battle of Armageddon will be considered as His sheep or the righteous and they will be separated from the goats (Matthew 25:31-46). This will include the 144,000 Israeli believers, and other Gentiles. They will maintain a natural body because they have not been resurrected and obtained glorified bodies.

> † Matthew 25: 31-46, *"³¹When the Son of man shall come in his glory, and all the holy angels with him, then shall he sit upon the throne of his glory: ³²And before him shall be gathered all nations: and he shall*

separate them one from another, as a shepherd divideth his sheep from the goats: ³³And he shall set the sheep on his right hand, but the goats on the left. ³⁴Then shall the King say unto them on his right hand, Come, ye blessed of my Father, inherit the kingdom prepared for you from the foundation of the world: ³⁵ For I was an hungred, and ye gave me meat: I was thirsty, and ye gave me drink: I was a stranger, and ye took me in: ³⁶Naked, and ye clothed me: I was sick, and ye visited me: I was in prison, and ye came unto me. ³⁷Then shall the righteous answer him, saying, Lord, when saw we thee an hungred, and fed thee? or thirsty, and gave thee drink? ³⁸When saw we thee a stranger, and took thee in? or naked, and clothed thee? ³⁹Or when saw we thee sick, or in prison, and came unto thee? ⁴⁰And the King shall answer and say unto them, Verily I say unto you, Inasmuch as ye have done it unto one of the least of these my brethren, ye have done it unto me. ⁴¹Then shall he say also unto them on the left hand, Depart from me, ye cursed, into everlasting fire, prepared for the devil and his angels: ⁴²For I was an hungred, and ye gave me no meat: I was thirsty, and ye gave me no drink: ⁴³ I was a stranger, and ye took me not in: naked, and ye clothed me not: sick, and in prison, and ye visited me not. ⁴⁴Then shall they also answer him, saying, Lord, when saw we thee an hungred, or athirst, or a stranger, or naked, or sick, or in prison, and did not minister unto thee? ⁴⁵Then shall he answer them, saying, Verily I say unto you, Inasmuch as ye did it not to one of the least of these, ye did it not to me. ⁴⁶And these shall go away into everlasting punishment: but the righteous into life eternal."

Isaiah 24:6 and Matthew 24:21-22 note that a few will survive and be left after the Battle of Armageddon. Zechariah 13:1 and Romans 11:26 reveal that many Jews, although they missed the Rapture, will place trust in Jesus and be saved. All Jews will not be saved but many will convert after the time of trouble.

† Isaiah 24:6, *"Therefore hath the curse devoured the earth, and they that dwell therein are desolate: therefore the inhabitants of the earth are burned, and few men left."*

† Zechariah 3:1, *"In that day there shall be a fountain opened to the house of David and to the inhabitants of Jerusalem for sin and for uncleanness."*

† Matthew 24:21-22, *"²¹For then shall be great tribulation, such as was not since the beginning of the world to this time, no, nor ever shall be. ²²And except those days should be shortened, there should no flesh be saved: but for the elect's sake those days shall be shortened."*

† Romans 11:26, *"And so all Israel shall be saved: as it is written, There shall come out of Sion the Deliverer, and shall turn away ungodliness from Jacob:"*

Believing Tribulation survivors which enter the Millennium will have mortal bodies and will procreate. There is no mention of another Rapture in Revelation 19-20 so it is best understood that the believers, alive on earth at the Second Coming, will go into the Millennium in their natural and non-glorified and non-resurrected bodies. Those who will have been resurrected and will have had glorified bodies cannot marry nor can they procreate. However, those with non-glorified or natural bodies will have children during the Millennium. Those with mortal bodies will have to choose whom they will serve. Yet, the enemy has been bound in the Abyss during the Millennium. When Satan gets released he will be allowed to deceive the nations. Some of those who were born during the Millennium will rebel against God just as did Adam and Eve in the Garden of Eden.

The Battle of Gog and Magog, the last battle, will begin at the ending of the Millennium.

† Revelation 20:7-9, *"⁷And when the thousand years are expired, Satan shall be loosed out of his prison, ⁸And shall go out to deceive the nations which are in the four quarters of the earth, Gog, and Magog, to gather them together to battle: the number of whom is as the sand of the sea. ⁹And they went up on the breadth of the earth, and compassed the camp of the saints about, and the beloved city: and fire came down from God out of heaven, and devoured them."*

RECOMMENDED ACTIVITIES

1. Study Romans 11:26 and determine what is meant by "all Israel". Consider using many commentaries, which can be found on www.studylight.org and www.biblehub.com.
2. Study Isaiah 65-66 alongside of Revelation 20-21.
3. Study calendar history. Many groups use various dates and years and therefore different calendars. Gregorian, Julian, Hindu, Buddhist, Islamic, Jewish, Roman, Persian, Chinese, Coptic, Ethiopian, Mayan and others you may find. The website https://www.timeanddate.com/calendar/jewish-calendar.html and https://allthatsinteresting.com/what-year-is-it is a good and simple place to start.

PERSONAL NOTES

CHAPTER FIFTEEN

THE BATTLE OF GOG AND MAGOG

The last battle on this earth will be the Battle of Gog and Magog. This battle will be an all-out attack against Israel, after which Satan will be cast into the Lake of Fire. It arises at the end of the Millennium when Satan is released from the pit where he has been bound during the Millennium. During the Millennium Satan will be bound and not be allowed to deceive anyone as he did before. Upon his release he will for the last time be allowed deceive the nations. At that time the Bible says in Revelation 20:7-8 that Satan will gather the nations to battle from the four corners of the earth. The reference is given to a battle called Gog and Magog.

† Revelation 20:2-3, *"²And he laid hold on the dragon, that old serpent, which is the Devil, and Satan, and bound him a thousand years, ³And cast him into the bottomless pit, and shut him up, and set a seal upon him, that he should deceive the nations no more, till the thousand years should be fulfilled: and after that he must be loosed a little season."*

✝ Revelation 20:8, *"And shall go out to deceive the nations which are in the four quarters of the earth, Gog, and Magog, to gather them together to battle: the number of whom is as the sand of the sea."*

The battle of Gog and Magog, found in both Ezekiel 38-39 and Revelation 20, is the source of much debate. There are many views on when the battle of Gog and Magog will take place. Below are some of the various arguments:

1. The battle of Ezekiel 38 and 39 are different.
2. The battle of Ezekiel 38-39 is the same as the one mentioned in Revelation 20.
3. The battle of Gog and Magog is the Battle of Armageddon.
4. The battle of Ezekiel 38-39 has already taken place.
5. The Revelation 20 Gog and Magog battle is an allusion to the Ezekiel battle.
6. There are two different battles; One in Ezekiel 38-39 and one in Revelation 20 occurring at different times in the end.

The comparison chart may help to evaluate the relationships of these Biblical passages.

COMPARISON OF EZEKIEL 38-39 AND REVELATION 20

ELEMENT	EZEKIEL 38-39	REVELATION 20
Initiator of the battle	God Ezekiel 38:1 ¹And the word of the LORD came unto me, saying, Ezekiel 39:1 ¹Therefore, thou son of man, prophesy against Gog, and say, Thus saith the Lord GOD; Behold, I am against thee, O Gog, the chief prince of Meshech and Tubal:	Satan Revelation 20:7-8 ⁷And when the thousand years are expired, Satan shall be loosed out of his prison, ⁸And shall go out to deceive the nations which are in the four quarters of the earth, Gog and Magog, to gather them together to battle: the number of whom is as the sand of the sea.
Gog-Magog	Gog – a person- the Chief Prince of Meshech and Tubal who rules over Magog (Russia) Magog- a land - Russia Magog, Meshech and Tubal were sons of Japheth who was the son of Noah. Ezekiel 38:2-3 ²Son of man, set thy face against Gog, the land of Magog, the chief prince of Meshech and Tubal, and prophesy against him, ³And say, Thus saith the Lord GOD; Behold, I am against thee, O Gog, the chief prince of Meshech and Tubal Ezekiel 39:1 (as above)	Unspecified Mentions Gog and Magog but in no specific relationship
Battlefield	Mount of Israel Ezekiel 38:8 ⁸After many days thou shalt be visited: in the latter years thou shalt come into the land that is brought back from the sword, and is gathered out of many people, against the mountains of Israel, which have been always waste: but it is brought forth out of the nations, and they shall dwell safely all of them. Ezekiel 39:2 ²And I will turn thee back, and leave but the sixth part of thee, and will cause thee to come up from the north parts, and will bring thee upon the mountains of Israel:	Jerusalem at end of Millennium Revelation 20: 7-8 (as above) Revelation 20:9 ⁹And they went up on the breadth of the earth, and compassed the camp of the saints about, and the beloved city: and fire came down from God out of heaven, and devoured them.
Attacked from	The North Parts-- involves several Middle Eastern nations Ezekiel 38:15 ¹⁵And thou shalt come from thy place out of the north parts, thou, and many people with thee, all of them riding upon horses, a great company, and a mighty army: Ezekiel 39:2 (as above	Four corners of the earth—involves nations from all over the world Revelation 20: 7-8 (as above)

Battle is against	Nation of Israel Ezekiel 38: 16 [16]And thou shalt come up against my people of Israel, as a cloud to cover the land; it shall be in the latter days, and I will bring thee against my land, that the heathen may know me, when I shall be sanctified in thee, O Gog, before their eyes.	God Uprising of those born during Millennium and deceived by Satan when he was released from prison. Satan will lead the battle to come against God one more time and then his final defeat. Revelation 20: 7-8 (as above)
Burial	Multitudes buried Burying the dead for 7 months. Dead are buried. Ezekiel 39:11-12 11And it shall come to pass in that day, that I will give unto Gog a place there of graves in Israel, the valley of the passengers on the east of the sea: and it shall stop the noses of the passengers: and there shall they bury Gog and all his multitude: and they shall call it The valley of Hamon–gog. 12And seven months shall the house of Israel be burying of them, that they may cleanse the land.	No burial but Satan is cast into lake of fire No need for a burial as the Great White Throne Judgment is upon them. Dead are devoured by fire. Revelation 20: 10 [10]And the devil that deceived them was cast into the lake of fire and brimstone, where the beast and the false prophet *are*, and shall be tormented day and night for ever and ever.
Post battle clean up	7 month clean up 7 years burning of weapons Ezekiel 39:11-12 (as above) Ezekiel 39:9 9And they that dwell in the cities of Israel shall go forth, and shall set on fire and burn the weapons, both the shields and the bucklers, the bows and the arrows, and the handstaves, and the spears, and they shall burn them with fire seven years:	No clean up is mentioned. There is no time for 7 years of burning weapons for the Great White Throne Judgment is upon them. This takes place at the end of the Millennium and before the Great White Throne Judgment. Revelation 20:11-15 [11]And I saw a great white throne, and him that sat on it, from whose face the earth and the heaven fled away; and there was found no place for them. [12]And I saw the dead, small and great, stand before God; and the books were opened: and another book was opened, which is *the book* of life: and the dead were judged out of those things which were written in the books, according to their works. [13]And the sea gave up the dead which were in it; and death and hell delivered up the dead which were in them: and they were judged every man according to their works. [14]And death and hell were cast into the lake of fire. This is the second death. [15]And whosoever was not found written in the book of life was cast into the lake of fire.
Satan	No mention of Satan in Ezekiel 38-39	Satan is released from prison goes out to deceive the nations and gathers them together for one last battle. Revelation 20: 7-8 (as above)

Purpose	Gog intends to overwhelm Israel but God uses this battle victory to bring Israel back to Him. Israel returns to God before the end of the Millennium. Israel at the end of the Millennium has been faithful 1000 years.	Satan uses a last effort to deceive the nations and gather for one last battle against God and His people. Revelation 20:7-10 (as above)
Israel	Israel must be prosperous, present in Israel and at peace in her land. Settled in old estates, at peace in unwalled villages and dwelling safely. Ezekiel 36:11 [11]And I will multiply upon you man and beast; and they shall increase and bring fruit: and I will settle you after your old estates, and will do better *unto you* than at your beginnings: and ye shall know that I *am* the LORD. Ezekiel 38:11 [11]And thou shalt say, I will go up to the land of unwalled villages; I will go to them that are at rest, that dwell safely, all of them dwelling without walls, and having neither bars nor gates,	Satan compassed the camp of the saints. He tries to deceive the nations not just Israel. Revelation 20:8-9 [8]And shall go out to deceive the nations which are in the four quarters of the earth, Gog and Magog, to gather them together to battle: the number of whom *is* as the sand of the sea. [9]And they went up on the breadth of the earth, and compassed the camp of the saints about, and the beloved city: and fire came down from God out of heaven, and devoured them.
Destroyed by	Earthquake Ezekiel 38:19 [19]For in my jealousy and in the fire of my wrath have I spoken, Surely in that day there shall be a great shaking in the land of Israel;	Fire from Heaven. God will intervene by pouring fire from the sky. Revelation 20:9 [9]And they went up on the breadth of the earth, and compassed the camp of the saints about, and the beloved city: and fire came down from God out of heaven, and devoured them.

From the comparison chart we can surmise that Ezekiel and Revelation are detailing different battles. Clearly there is a battle of Gog and Magog at the end of the Millennium as stated in Revelation 20:7-8. The considerations of Ezekiel 38-39 seem to indicate conceivably there is another battle just before or at the beginning of the Tribulation time. While not all agree there is a second Gog and Magog war at the end of Millennium, many scholars agree there is an Ezekiel 38-39 battle just before the Tribulation or at the beginning of it.

It seems logical for this battle to be after the Rapture or at the beginning of the Tribulation, especially considering the timeframe of a seven-year period for clean up. The battle of Ezekiel 38-39 points to a Russia and Middle Eastern war. This war must happen before the Millennium because Islam cannot enter the Millennium and Israel will have already been saved.

The prophecy in Ezekiel 38-39 considers the armies from the north in Ezekiel 38-39's future invasion (Ezekiel 38:1-6). Ezekiel gives us some ancient names for a Russian-Middle Eastern (Islamic) alliance.

† Ezekiel 38:1-6, *"¹And the word of the LORD came unto me, saying, ²Son of man, set thy face against Gog, the land of Magog, the chief prince of Meshech and Tubal, and prophesy against him, ³And say, Thus saith the Lord GOD; Behold, I am against thee, O Gog, the chief prince of Meshech and Tubal: ⁴And I will turn thee back, and put hooks into thy jaws, and I will bring thee forth, and all thine army, horses and horsemen, all of them clothed with all sorts of armour, even a great company with bucklers and shields, all of them handling swords: ⁵Persia, Ethiopia, and Libya with them; all of them with shield and helmet: ⁶Gomer, and all his bands; the house of Togarmah of the north quarters, and all his bands: and many people with thee."*

Gog refers to a powerful leader of an end time's northern coalition between Russia and the Middle East. Gog may be a name or a title. He is referred to as the "Prince of Rosh". Rosh is a son of Benjamin as seen in Genesis 46:21, "And the sons of Benjamin *were* Belah, and Becher, and Ashbel, Gera, and Naaman, Ehi, and Rosh, Muppim, and Huppim, and Ard." Rosh is believed by many to be Russia, as one of the three ancient Scythian tribes. The word Rosh means bitter or poisonous herb or venom. It is also a common Hebrew word for *chief* or *head*.

We have to trace the children of Noah to identify the other names in the text. Noah had three sons: Japheth, Shem and Ham. Japheth had seven sons, of which, four are mentioned here: Magog, Gomer, Tubal and Meshech. After the tower of Babel, the Japhetic race moved to East Europe and what we know as modern-day Russia. Magog refers to a Russia Federation and former Soviet Union republics. (The "stans" like Uzbekistan, Kazakhstan and so forth). Meshech, Tubal, Gomer and the house of Togarmah are Turkey. Persia is now Iran. Ham is the father of

Put and Cush. Put is Libya and Cush is Ethiopia and possibly Central African nations. These nations in the battle described in Ezekiel 38-39 will align with Russia, the King of the North. The King of the South refers to the African-Arab coalition. The purpose is to destroy Israel (Ezekiel 38:12-16) however, the Lord will intervene and defend Israel and all will know that He is the Lord (Ezekiel 38:23).

REFERENCED SCRIPTURES

† Genesis 10:2-3, "*²The sons of Japheth; Gomer, and Magog, and Madai, and Javan, and Tubal, and Meshech, and Tiras. ³And the sons of Gomer; Ashkenaz, and Riphath, and Togarmah.*"

† Genesis 10:6, "*And the sons of Ham; Cush, and Mizraim, and Put, and Canaan.*"

† Ezekiel 38:12-16, "*¹²To take a spoil, and to take a prey; to turn thine hand upon the desolate places that are now inhabited, and upon the people that are gathered out of the nations, which have gotten cattle and goods, that dwell in the midst of the land.¹³Sheba, and Dedan, and the merchants of Tarshish, with all the young lions thereof, shall say unto thee, Art thou come to take a spoil? hast thou gathered thy company to take a prey? to carry away silver and gold, to take away cattle and goods, to take a great spoil? ¹⁴Therefore, son of man, prophesy and say unto Gog, Thus saith the Lord GOD; In that day when my people of Israel dwelleth safely, shalt thou not know it? ¹⁵And thou shalt come from thy place out of the north parts, thou, and many people with thee, all of them riding upon horses, a great company, and a mighty army: ¹⁶And thou shalt come up against my people of Israel, as a cloud to cover the land; it shall be in the latter days, and I will bring thee against my land, that the heathen may know me, when I shall be sanctified in thee, O Gog, before their eyes.*"

† Ezekiel 38:23, "*Thus will I magnify myself, and sanctify myself; and I will be known in the eyes of many nations, and they shall know that I am the LORD.*

What we can conclude is there will be three end time wars.

1. War of Ezekiel 38-39. The future invasion of Israel as we discussed. This is the war whereby Israel will return to God and must occur before the Tribulation.
2. Battle of Armageddon. This is the battle whereby the Antichrist and False Prophet will be seized thrown alive into the Lake of Fire. This was discussed in a previous chapter.
3. Battle of Gog and Magog of Revelation 20. The last and final rebellion against God. This war will occur at the end of the Millennium.

THREE END TIMES WARS SUMMARIZED

WAR	SCRIPTURE	SUMMARY
1. Invasion of Israel	Ezekiel 38-39	• This war could not occur until Israel was restored as a nation in 1948 • Armies from the North invade Israel • Occurs before the Tribulation- Near the time of the Rapture • Israel aligned for her end time purpose • Israel returns to God
2. Battle of Armageddon	Revelation 16:12-16 Revelation 19:11-21	• All nations involved • Bloodiest battle in history • Jesus Christ will capture the Antichrist and the False Prophet and throw them into the Lake of Fire • Occurs at the end of the Tribulation at the Second Coming of Christ
3. Battle of Gog and Magog	Revelation 20:7-8	• Satan comes against God and His saints one last time • Satan released and goes to all four corners of the earth and deceives many • Occurs at the end of the Millennium just before the Great White Throne Judgment • Satan will be cast into the Lake of Fire • Will take place in Israel

It can be very difficult to sort out what is truth when studying Biblical resources, especially on the Internet. Many have different opinions, beliefs, and interpretations. Be cognizant of and stay clear of false teachings and false prophets (2 Peter 2:1; 1John 4:1). Do your best to search the scriptures and study the Word of God. The Word of God interprets itself. Be certain that your resources line up with the Word of God. Remember too, that God only gave us an overview of the end times and therefore we cannot be dogmatic about its study. He has not revealed all things as John wrote in Revelation 10:4.

REFERENCED SCRIPTURES

† Second Peter 2:1, *"But there were false prophets also among the people, even as there shall be false teachers among you, who privily shall bring in damnable heresies, even denying the Lord that bought them, and bring upon themselves swift destruction."*

† First John 4:1, *"Beloved, believe not every spirit, but try the spirits whether they are of God: because many false prophets are gone out into the world."*

† Revelation 10:4, *"And when the seven thunders had uttered their voices, I was about to write: and I heard a voice from heaven saying unto me, Seal up those things which the seven thunders uttered, and write them not."*

PERSONAL NOTES

CHAPTER SIXTEEN

THE GREAT WHITE THRONE JUDGMENT

† Revelation 20:11-15, *"¹¹And I saw a great white throne, and him that sat on it, from whose face the earth and the heaven fled away; and there was found no place for them. ¹²And I saw the dead, small and great, stand before God; and the books were opened: and another book was opened, which is the book of life: and the dead were judged out of those things which were written in the books, according to their works. ¹³And the sea gave up the dead which were in it; and death and hell delivered up the dead which were in them: and they were judged every man according to their works. ¹⁴And death and hell were cast into the lake of fire. This is the second death. ¹⁵And whosoever was not found written in the book of life was cast into the lake of fire."*

A loving God loved us so much that He has given warning after warning and pricked and nudged the hearts of people time after time. He loved us so much that He died on the cross at Calvary to bring about redemption and offered life rather than death. He loved us so much that He spoke to about forty men over at least 1500 years to give us His Word, the Bible. He loved us so much that He called men and women to minister the Word into the hearts of mankind. He loved us so much that He allowed many uncomfortable circumstances to come our way to cause us to realize there must be someone greater than ourselves. He loved us so much that He gave us His plan for the world affirming that He would return to separate those who accepted and followed Him from those who denied Him. That loving God will soon perform His wrath upon those who have rejected Him. The final wrath is called the last judgment and more specifically, the Great White Throne Judgment. This is the time for those who denied Him to be separated forever from God and they will be placed into the Lake of Fire. There will be no further opportunity to be redeemed, saved, or forgiven of sin. There will be no further opportunity to experience His boundless and amazing love. There will be no further opportunity to call upon Him for help in times of trouble. Those who died without a true relationship with Jesus Christ will experience The Great White Throne Judgment. The secrets of men will be revealed in the day when God judges (Romans 2:16). This is the second death for the non-believer. Eternity will be in the Lake of Fire forever where there will be wailing and gnashing of teeth, fire and brimstone (sulfur), and no rest day or night.

REFERENCED SCRIPTURES

† Matthew 10:28, *"And fear not them which kill the body, but are not able to kill the soul: but rather fear him which is able to destroy both soul and body in hell."*

† Matthew 13:42, *"And shall cast them into a furnace of fire: there shall be wailing and gnashing of teeth."*

† Luke 16:19-28, *"[19]There was a certain rich man, which was clothed in purple and fine linen, and fared sumptuously every day: [20]And there was a certain beggar named Lazarus, which was laid at his*

gate, full of sores, ²¹And desiring to be fed with the crumbs which fell from the rich man's table: moreover the dogs came and licked his sores. ²²And it came to pass, that the beggar died, and was carried by the angels into Abraham's bosom: the rich man also died, and was buried; ²³And in hell he lift up his eyes, being in torments, and seeth Abraham afar off, and Lazarus in his bosom. ²⁴And he cried and said, Father Abraham, have mercy on me, and send Lazarus, that he may dip the tip of his finger in water, and cool my tongue; for I am tormented in this flame. ²⁵But Abraham said, Son, remember that thou in thy lifetime receivedst thy good things, and likewise Lazarus evil things: but now he is comforted, and thou art tormented. ²⁶And beside all this, between us and you there is a great gulf fixed: so that they which would pass from hence to you cannot; neither can they pass to us, that would come from thence. ²⁷Then he said, I pray thee therefore, father, that thou wouldest send him to my father's house: ²⁸For I have five brethren; that he may testify unto them, lest they also come into this place of torment."

† Romans 2:16, "In the day when God shall judge the secrets of men by Jesus Christ according to my gospel."

† Revelation 14:10-11, "¹⁰The same shall drink of the wine of the wrath of God, which is poured out without mixture into the cup of his indignation; and he shall be tormented with fire and brimstone in the presence of the holy angels, and in the presence of the Lamb: ¹¹And the smoke of their torment ascendeth up for ever and ever: and they have no rest day nor night, who worship the beast and his image, and whosoever receiveth the mark of his name."

Believers will not be judged at The Great White Throne Judgment. Refer back to the chapter concerning deaths and resurrections. They will receive rewards at the Judgment Seat or Bema Seat as we have already discussed. The phrase, *Great White Throne Judgment*, refers to the day when Christ Jesus Himself will sit on His Throne and bring justice to those who denied Him. All unrighteousness will be judged. God is a just God and that means He will judge fairly and impartially. He will not be biased to the great or to the small or to the rich or poor. Not everyone that calls on the name of the Lord will enter heaven because He is just. He knows those that have a true relationship with Him from those who just talk the talk (Matthew 7:21-23).

> † Mathew 7:21-23, *"²¹Not every one that saith unto me, Lord, Lord, shall enter into the kingdom of heaven; but he that doeth the will of my Father which is in heaven. ²²Many will say to me in that day, Lord, Lord, have we not prophesied in thy name? and in thy name have cast out devils? and in thy name done many wonderful works? ²³And then will I profess unto them, I never knew you: depart from me, ye that work iniquity."*

The unjust will stand before God as He opens the *Book of Life*. Jesus mentions the *Book of Life* as He talks to His disciples in Luke 10:20. Paul declared that the names of his fellow workers were written in the *Book of Life*. This book contains the names of those who have accepted Christ as Lord and Savior, have confessed sins, and followed the way of Jesus. Some infer that our name is written into the *Book of Life* when we accept Christ. Others suppose that our name is written at birth and will be blotted out at the Day of Judgment for those who did not accept Christ as Lord (Revelation 3:5). I believe this to be the case. Whichever the circumstance, the result is the same. The non-believer will be cast into the Lake of Fire.

Revelation 20:12 signifies that the works of the non-believer are documented and they will be judged according to their works. Salvation is not earned by works but by grace through faith (Ephesians 2:8). As we discussed, believers will be rewarded according to their works. Believers receive rewards based on what was done for Christ. The same principle applies to the non-believer who will be sentenced to the Lake of Fire for their non-belief and their evil works or lack of work for the Lord. There are different degrees of punishment depending on the degrees of evil works (Luke 12:42-48).

REFERENCED SCRIPTURES

✝ Luke 10:20, "Notwithstanding in this rejoice not, that the spirits are subject unto you; but rather rejoice, because your names are written in heaven."

✝ Luke 12:42-48, "[42]And the Lord said, Who then is that faithful and wise steward, whom his lord shall make ruler over his household, to give them their portion of meat in due season? [43]Blessed is that servant, whom his lord when he cometh shall find so doing. [44]Of a truth I say unto you, that he will make him ruler over all that he hath. [45]But and if that servant say in his heart, My lord delayeth his coming; and shall begin to beat the menservants and maidens, and to eat and drink, and to be drunken; [46]The lord of that servant will come in a day when he looketh not for him, and at an hour when he is not aware, and will cut him in sunder, and will appoint him his portion with the unbelievers. [47]And that servant, which knew his lord's will, and prepared not himself, neither did according to his will, shall be beaten with many stripes. [48]But he that knew not, and did commit things worthy of stripes, shall be beaten with few stripes. For unto whomsoever much is given, of him shall be much required: and to whom men have committed much, of him they will ask the more."

✝ Ephesians 2:8, "For by grace are ye saved through faith; and that not of yourselves: it is the gift of God:"

✝ Philippians 4:3, "And I intreat thee also, true yokefellow, help those women which laboured with me in the gospel, with Clement also, and with other my fellowlabourers, whose names are in the book of life."

✝ Revelation 3:5, "He that overcometh, the same shall be clothed in white raiment; and I will not blot out his name out of the book of life, but I will confess his name before my Father, and before his angels."

✝ Revelation 20:11-15, "[11]And I saw a great white throne, and him that sat on it, from whose face the earth and the heaven fled away; and there was found no place for them. [12]And I saw the dead, small and great, stand before God; and the books were opened: and another book was opened, which is the book of life: and the dead were judged out of those things which were written in the books, according to their *works. [13]And the sea gave up the dead which were in it; and death and hell delivered up the dead which were in them: and they were judged every man according to their works. [14]And death and hell were cast into the lake of fire. This is the second death. [15]And whosoever was not found written in the book of life was cast into the lake of fire."*

We hear a lot about justice. People want justice. There are projects in the name of justice. When wrong is done to someone, there is a cry for justice. Protestors and rioters say they call for justice. There is even a comic book crying for justice. Some want moral justice, religious justice, or legal justice. At the Great White Throne Judgment, real justice will finally be served. What a sad day! If only people would hear the truth, believe, confess their sins and repent! Do it now before it is too late.

PERSONAL NOTES

CHAPTER SEVENTEEN

THE NEW HEAVEN AND NEW EARTH

The Apostle John experienced a concluding vision of the new heaven and new earth. Heaven will include a new city called the New Jerusalem, which will come down out of heaven from God (Revelation 21:9-10). The old earth full of sin, suffering and sickness will be destroyed. All of creation has been groaning as it waits for this glorious day (Romans 8:22). Next... finally... there will be a new heaven and a new earth (Isaiah 65:17, Isaiah 66:22; 2 Peter 3:13, Revelation 21:1). This event follows the Great White Throne Judgment when God will make all things new.

Some refer to a regenerated heaven and earth. I choose to believe that new means new and not regenerated. New means that it never existed before. Furthermore, the scripture says that the first heaven and earth were passed away (Revelation 21:1). God will make all things new. The old will pass away. We will dwell with the Lord worshipping Him for eternity in our glorified bodies.

The Bible teaches us only a little about the new heaven and new earth. There will be a river of life but there will be no more sea (Revelation 21:1). Some may consider why will there be no more sea. The sea in our day embodies an image of majestic beauty and recreation. However, in the ancient world the sea embodied that which was evil, threatening and chaotic. Notice that the beast of Revelation 13: 1-2 comes out of the sea. While there will be no more sea there will be a life-giving river. Yet, In the Eden of past there were four rivers: Pishon, Gihon, Hiddekel also known as Tigris, and Euphrates (Genesis 2:10-14). The river of water of life in Revelation flows from the throne of God to His people (Psalms 46:4, Revelation 22:1). It represents the eternal life we have as believers in Christ Jesus.

In the new heaven and earth all tears will be wiped away (Revelation 7:17; Revelation 21:4). There will be no sorrow, no crying and no pain. When the scriptures talk about no more tears it is in the context of the future new heaven and new earth it makes me wonder about tears in the current heaven. Why would the Lord tell us He will wipe tears from our eyes in the future heaven and earth if we have been in heaven, had put on our glorified bodies, and have lived in the Millennial Kingdom for 1000 years with Him? Why would He have to wipe away our tears after all of this? Do they cry in heaven now? Maybe there are tears when someone dies without knowing the Lord. Maybe there will be tears in heaven for those during the Tribulation. Maybe there are tears of joy when someone gets saved. Perhaps there are tears of regret for lost opportunities.

There will be freedom from conflicts, temptations, and suffering. There will be no more sin and evil. Death, sorrow, and mourning will cease (Isaiah 51:11; Isaiah 65:19; Revelation 21:1-8).

No longer will there be any curse. God placed a curse on creation when Adam and Eve sinned in the Garden of Eden (Genesis 3:14-19). That curse will be lifted in the new heaven and new earth.

The city will display the glory of God. It will be positioned like a cube. It will measure about 12,000 furlongs, which is about 1500 miles in length, width, and height. One furlong is 0.125 miles. California's coastline is 840 miles long. Texas is about 760 miles long and 660 miles wide. Alaska is 1,400 miles long and 2,700 miles wide. Compare this for yourself! Amazing isn't it? The wall will be approximately 216 feet thick! The walls will be made of jasper and decorated with precious stones like jasper, sapphire, agate, emerald, onyx, ruby, jacinth, and amethyst. The city will have a great street made of gold and will look like translucent glass. Notice it says a great street (singular) not streets (plural). The light will shine like most precious stones of jasper and clear as crystal. There will be no more night and no more darkness. Light reveals and darkness hides. There will be no need for the sun for Christ will be our light, the only lamp we will need. He will illuminate all of heaven and earth with His glory.

There will be a great wall with twelve gates and twelve assigned angels with names of the twelve tribes. The twelve foundations will have the names of the twelve apostles written on them.

This is the day that all believers long for. This is the hope that we have in Him!

REFERENCED SCRIPTURES

† Genesis 2:10-14, "¹⁰ And a river went out of Eden to water the garden; and from thence it was parted, and became into four heads. ¹¹The name of the first is Pison: that is it which compasseth the whole land of Havilah, where there is gold; ¹²And the gold of that land is good: there is bdellium and the onyx stone. ¹³And the name of the second river is Gihon: the same is it that compasseth the whole land of Ethiopia. ¹⁴And the name of the third river is Hiddekel: that is it which goeth toward the east of Assyria. And the fourth river is Euphrates.

✝ Genesis 3:14-19, *"¹⁴And the L*ORD *God said unto the serpent, Because thou hast done this, thou art cursed above all cattle, and above every beast of the field; upon thy belly shalt thou go, and dust shalt thou eat all the days of thy life: ¹⁵And I will put enmity between thee and the woman, and between thy seed and her seed; it shall bruise thy head, and thou shalt bruise his heel. ¹⁶Unto the woman he said, I will greatly multiply thy sorrow and thy conception; in sorrow thou shalt bring forth children; and thy desire shall be to thy husband, and he shall rule over thee. ¹⁷And unto Adam he said, Because thou hast hearkened unto the voice of thy wife, and hast eaten of the tree, of which I commanded thee, saying, Thou shalt not eat of it: cursed is the ground for thy sake; in sorrow shalt thou eat of it all the days of thy life; "¹⁸Thorns also and thistles shall it bring forth to thee; and thou shalt eat the herb of the field; ¹⁹In the sweat of thy face shalt thou eat bread, till thou return unto the ground; for out of it wast thou taken: for dust thou art, and unto dust shalt thou return."*

✝ Psalms 46:4, *"There is a river, the streams whereof shall make glad the city of God, the holy place of the tabernacles of the most High."*

✝ Isaiah 51:11, *"Therefore the redeemed of the L*ORD *shall return, and come with singing unto Zion; and everlasting joy shall be upon their head: they shall obtain gladness and joy; and sorrow and mourning shall flee away."*

✝ Isaiah 65:17, *"For, behold, I create new heavens and a new earth: and the former shall not be remembered, nor come into mind."*

✝ Isaiah 66:22, *"For as the new heavens and the new earth, which I will make, shall remain before me, saith the LORD, so shall your descendants and your name remain."*

✝ Romans 8:22, *"For we know that the whole creation groaneth and travaileth in pain together until now."*

✝ Second Peter 3:13, *"Nevertheless we, according to his promise, look for new heavens and a new earth, wherein dwelleth righteousness."*

✝ Revelation 7:17, *"For the Lamb which is in the midst of the throne shall feed them, and shall lead them unto living fountains of waters: and God shall wipe away all tears from their eyes."*

✝ Revelation 21:1-8, "*¹And I saw a new heaven and a new earth: for the first heaven and the first earth were passed away; and there was no more sea. ²And I John saw the holy city, new Jerusalem, coming down from God out of heaven, prepared as a bride adorned for her husband. ³And I heard a great voice out of heaven saying, Behold, the tabernacle of God is with men, and he will dwell with them, and they shall be his people, and God himself shall be with them, and be their God. ⁴And God shall wipe away all tears from their eyes; and there shall be no more death, neither sorrow, nor crying, neither shall there be any more pain: for the former things are passed away. ⁵And he that sat upon the throne said, Behold, I make all things new. And he said unto me, Write: for these words are true and faithful. ⁶And he said unto me, It is done. I am Alpha and Omega, the beginning and the end. I will give unto him that is athirst of the fountain of the water of life freely. ⁷He that overcometh shall inherit all things; and I will be his God, and he shall be my son. ⁸But the fearful, and unbelieving, and the abominable, and murderers, and whoremongers, and sorcerers, and idolaters, and all liars, shall have their part in the lake which burneth with fire and brimstone: which is the second death.*

✝ Revelation 21:9-10, "*⁹And there came unto me one of the seven angels which had the seven vials full of the seven last plagues, and talked with me, saying, Come hither, I will shew thee the bride, the Lamb's wife. ¹⁰And he carried me away in the spirit to a great and high mountain, and shewed me that great city, the holy Jerusalem, descending out of heaven from God,*"

✝ Revelation 21:15-27, "*¹⁵And he that talked with me had a golden reed to measure the city, and the gates thereof, and the wall thereof. ¹⁶And the city lieth foursquare, and the length is as large as the breadth: and he measured the city with the reed, twelve thousand furlongs. The length and the breadth and the height of it are equal. ¹⁷And he measured the wall thereof, an hundred and forty and four cubits, according to the measure of a man, that is, of the angel. ¹⁸And the building of the wall of it was of jasper: and the city was pure gold, like unto clear glass. ¹⁹And the foundations of the wall of the city were garnished with all manner of precious stones. The first* *foundation was jasper; the second, sapphire; the third, a chalcedony; the fourth, an emerald; ²⁰The fifth, sardonyx; the sixth, sardius; the seventh, chrysolyte; the eighth, beryl; the ninth, a topaz; the tenth, a chrysoprasus; the eleventh, a jacinth; the twelfth, an amethyst. ²¹And the twelve gates were twelve pearls: every several gate was of one pearl: and the street of the city was pure gold, as it were transparent glass. ²²And I saw no temple therein: for the Lord God Almighty and the Lamb are the temple of it. ²³And the city had no need of the sun, neither of the moon, to shine in it: for the glory of God did lighten it, and the Lamb is the light thereof. ²⁴And the nations of them which are saved shall walk in the light of it: and the kings of the earth do bring their glory and honour into it. ²⁵And the gates of it shall not be shut at all by day: for there shall be no night there. ²⁶And they shall bring the glory and honour of the nations into it. ²⁷And there shall in no wise enter into it any thing that defileth, neither whatsoever worketh abomination, or maketh a lie: but they which are written in the Lamb's book of life."*

† Revelation 22:1-5, "*¹And he shewed me a pure river of water of life, clear as crystal, proceeding out of the throne of God and of the Lamb. ²In the midst of the street of it, and on either side of the river, was there the tree of life, which bare twelve manner of fruits, and yielded her fruit every month: and the leaves of the tree were for the healing of the nations. ³And there shall be no more curse: but the throne of God and of the Lamb shall be in it; and his servants shall serve him: ⁴And they shall see his face; and his name shall be in their foreheads. ⁵And there shall be no night there; and they need no candle, neither light of the sun; for the Lord God giveth them light: and they shall reign for ever and ever.*"

There are many things that will no longer be in the new heaven and new earth as discussed. Here is a chart to echo the profoundness of 'NO MORE'!

NO MORE	REVELATION REFERENCE
No more sea	21:1, "and there was no more sea."
No more tears	21:4, "And God shall wipe away all tears from their eyes;"
No more death	21:4, "there shall be no more death"
No more sorrow	21:4, "neither sorrow"
No more crying	21:4, "nor crying"
No more pain	21:4, "neither shall there be any more pain:"
No more temple	21:22, "And I saw no temple therein: for the Lord God Almighty and the Lamb are the temple of it."
No more sun	21:23, "And the city had no need of the sun," 22:5, "And there shall be no night there; and they need no candle, neither light of the sun;"
No more moon	21:23, "neither of the moon, to shine in it: for the glory of God did lighten it, and the Lamb is the light thereof."
No more night	21:25, "or there shall be no night there." 22:5, "And there shall be no night there; and they need no candle, neither light of the sun;"
No more curse	22:3, "And there shall be no more curse:"

RECOMMENDED ACTIVITIES

1. Construct your own creative chart. Describe what the Bible says about heaven and compare what it says about hell.
2. If you have not already done so, choose where you would like to live in eternity. Make it official. Believe that Jesus is Lord and that He died for your redemption. Confess your sins in prayer. If you have done this then ask God to direct your path to the right Bible believing church. Commit to daily Bible reading and prayer along with praise and worship. Ask God to open the

spiritual eyes of your heart to His ways and His will. Walk with Him and talk with Him. He will reveal Himself to you in ways you have never imagined. He will never leave you nor forsake you. One day we will meet in heaven. This is the expectation of all who believe. This is the hope we have in Christ.

✝ Matthew 6:24, "No man can serve two masters: for either he will hate the one, and love the other; or else he will hold to the one, and despise the other. Ye cannot serve God and mammon."

✝ Romans 10:9, "That if thou shalt confess with thy mouth the Lord Jesus, and shalt believe in thine heart that God hath raised him from the dead, thou shalt be saved."

✝ First John 1:9, "If we confess our sins, he is faithful and just to forgive us *our* sins, and to cleanse us from all unrightcousncss."

PERSONAL NOTES

RECOMMENDED READING

Barclay, William. *The Revelation of John*. Philadelphia: Westminster Press, 1976.

Bickel, Bruce and Stan Jantz. *Bruce & Stan's Guide to the End of the World: A User Friendly Approach*. Oregon: Harvest House, 1999.

Bullinger, E.W. *Number in Scripture: Its Supernatural Design and Spiritual Significance*. Grand Rapids: Kregel Publications, 1967.

Cerullo, Morris. *End Time Prophecy Revelation Unveiled*. San Diego: Morris Cerullo World Evangelism, 1995.

Conner, Kevin J. and Ken Malmin. *Interpreting the Scripture: A Textbook on How to Interpret the Bible*. Portland: City Bible Publishing, 1983.

Duck, Daymond R. and Larry Richards. *The Book of Daniel: The Smart Guide to the Bible Series*. Nashville: Nelson Reference, 2007.

Duck, Daymond R. and Larry Richards. *The Book of Revelation: The Smart Guide to the Bible Series*. Nashville: Nelson Reference, 2006.

Greene, Oliver B. *The Revelation: Verse by Verse Study*. Greenville: Oliver B. Greene, 1963.

Hagee, John. *Jerusalem Countdown: A Warning to the World*. Little Mary: FrontLine, 2006.

Jeremiah, David. *Escape the Coming Night*. Dallas: Word Publishing, 1990.

Larkin, Clarence. *The Book of Revelation*. New York: Rev. Clarence Larkin, 1919.

Page, Mary L. *Blessings in the Book: A Study Guide for the Book of Revelation*. Fontana: CLF Publishing, 2016.

Rose Publishing. Rose Book of Charts, Maps, and Timelines. Shenzhen: Regent Publishing Services, Ltd., 2012.

Strong, James. *The New Strong's Exhaustive Concordance of the Bible*. Nashville: Thomas Nelson Publishers, 1990.

Tenney, Merrill C. *Interpreting Revelation*. Grand Rapids: Wm. B Eerdmans Publishing, 1957.

Josephus. *Josephus: The Complete Works*. Translated by William Whiston. Nashville: Thomas Nelson Publishers, 1998.

USEFUL WEBSITES

http://jewishencyclopedia.com/

http://timeline.biblehistory.com/home

http://www.biblebelievers.org.au/number01.htm

http://www.earnestlycontendingforthefaith.com/Books/
Clarence%20Larkin/Revelation/ClarenceLarkinTheBookOf
Revelation01.html

http://www.jewfaq.org/calendar.htm

http://www.lookinguntojesus.info/BSTopics/AncientNames
withCurrentNames.html

http://www.thewordnotes.com/numvalhg.pdf

https://allthatsinteresting.com/what-year-is-it

https://hebrew4christians.com/Holidays/Introduction/introduction.
html

https://philologos.org/__eb-nis/default.htm

https://sacred-texts.com/

https://www.artofmanliness.com/articles/how-to-gird-up-your-
loins-an-illustrated-guide/

https:// www.bbea.org/

https://www.bibleblender.com/2015/biblical-lessons/biblical-history/
list-of-bible-places-old-new-testament-biblical-locations

https://www.biblegateway.com/

https://www.bible-history.com/

https://www.biblehub.com/

https://www.blueletterbible.org/study/larkin/dt/10.cfm

https://www.biblestudytools.com/

https://www.billmounce.com/greekalphabet/greek-alphabet

https://www.chabad.org/library/article_cdo/aid/526874/jewish/The-
Jewish-Month.htm

https://www.davidjeremiah.org/

https://www.hebrew4christians.com/Grammar/Unit_One/Aleph-
Bet/aleph-bet.html

https://www.jewishvirtuallibrary.org/

https://www.jhm.org

https://www.levendwater.org/books/numbers/number_in_
scripture_bullinger.pdf

https://menorah-bible.jimdofree.com/english/structure-of-the-bible/
alphabets-and-numerical-values/

https://www.studylight.org/

https://www.timeanddate.com/calendar/

https://www.wogim.org/anland.htm

https://www.worldatlas.com/

Printed in the United States
By Bookmasters